DATE DUE

DEMCO 38-296

Two-Year College Mathematics Library Recommendations

Lynn Arthur Steen, Editor

THE MATHEMATICAL ASSOCIATION OF AMERICA

A Notes and Reports Series

started in 1982, addresses a broad range of topics and themes of interest to all who ...matics. The volumes in this series are readable, informative, and useful, and help the developments of importance to mathematics.

MAA Notes

1. Problem Solving in the Mathematics Curriculum,
   Committee on the Teaching of Undergraduate Mathematics,
   a subcommittee of the Committee on the Undergraduate Program in Mathematics, *Alan H. Schoenfeld,* Editor.

2. Recommendations on the Mathematical Preparation of Teachers,
   Committee on the Undergraduate Program in Mathematics, Panel on Teacher Training.

3. Undergraduate Mathematics Education in the People's Republic of China,
   Lynn A. Steen, Editor.

4. Notes on Primality Testing and Factoring,
   Carl Pomerance.

5. American Perspectives on the Fifth International Congress on Mathematical Education,
   Warren Page, Editor.

6. Toward a Lean and Lively Calculus,
   Ronald G. Douglas, Editor.

7. Undergraduate Programs in the Mathematical and Computer Sciences: 1985–86,
   D. J. Albers, R. D. Anderson, D. O. Loftsgaarden, Editors.

8. Calculus for a New Century,
   Lynn A. Steen, Editor.

9. Computers and Mathematics: The Use of Computers in Undergraduate Instruction,
   Committee on Computers in Mathematics Education, D. A. Smith, G. J. Porter, L. C. Leinbach, and R. H. Wenger, Editors.

10. Guidelines for the Continuing Mathematical Education of Teachers,
    Committee on the Mathematical Education of Teachers.

11. Keys to Improved Instruction by Teaching Assistants and Part-Time Instructors,
    Committee on Teaching Assistants and Part-Time Instructors, Bettye Anne Case, Editor.

12. The Use of Calculators in the Standardized Testing of Mathematics,
    John Kenelly, Editor, published jointly with The College Board.

13. Reshaping College Mathematics,
    Committee on the Undergraduate Program in Mathematics, Lynn A. Steen, Editor.

14. Mathematical Writing,
    by *Donald E. Knuth, Tracy Larrabee, and Paul M. Roberts.*

15. Discrete Mathematics in the First Two Years,
    Anthony Ralston, Editor.

16. Using Writing to Teach Mathematics,
    Andrew Sterrett, Editor.

17. Priming the Calculus Pump: Innovations and Resources,
    Committee on Calculus Reform and the First Two Years,
    a subcommittee of the Committee on the Undergraduate Program in Mathematics, *Thomas W. Tucker,* Editor.

18. Models for Undergraduate Research in Mathematics,
Lester Senechal, Editor.

19. Visualization in Teaching and Learning Mathematics,
Committee on Computers in Mathematics Education, Steve Cunningham and Walter S. Zimmermann, Editors.

20. The Laboratory Approach to Teaching Calculus,
L. Carl Leinbach et al., Editors.

21. Perspectives on Contemporary Statistics,
David C. Hoaglin and David S. Moore, Editors.

MAA Reports

1. A Curriculum in Flux: Mathematics at Two-Year Colleges,
Subcommittee on Mathematics Curriculum at Two-Year Colleges, a joint committee of the MAA and the American Mathematical Association of Two-Year Colleges, *Ronald M. Davis,* Editor.

2. A Source Book for College Mathematics Teaching,
Committee on the Teaching of Undergraduate Mathematics, Alan H. Schoenfeld, Editor.

3. A Call for Change: Recommendations for the Mathematical Preparation of Teachers of Mathematics,
Committee on the Mathematical Education of Teachers, James R. C. Leitzel, Editor.

4. Library Recommendations for Undergraduate Mathematics,
CUPM ad hoc Subcommittee, Lynn A. Steen, Editor.

5. Two-Year College Mathematics Library Recommendations,
CUPM ad hoc Subcommittee, Lynn A. Steen, Editor.

First Printing
© 1992 by the Mathematical Association of America
ISBN 0-88385-077-X
Printed in the United States of America

Table of Contents

Preface .... *v*

Reviewers .... *ix*

1 General 1
General Anthologies 1
Elementary Exposition 1
Advanced Surveys 2
Mathematics Appreciation Texts 3
Fiction, Aphorisms, Epigrams 3
Miscellany 3

2 Reference 4
Dictionaries 4
Handbooks 4
Encyclopedias 4
Bibliographies 4
Indexes 5

3 History 5
Surveys 5
Biographies 6
Source Books 7
Classic Works 7
Ancient and Medieval 7
Modern 8
Numbers and Algebra 8
Calculus and Analysis 8
Geometry 9
Probability and Statistics 9
Computers 9

4 Recreational Mathematics 9
Surveys 9
Games and Puzzles 10
Puzzle Collections 10
Contests and Problems 10
Martin Gardner 11
Miscellany 11

5 Education 11
Policy 11

Philosophy 12
Psychology 12
Culture 12
History 12
Curriculum and Instruction 12
Elementary Education 13
Secondary Education 14
Undergraduate Education 14
Minorities and Women 15
Problem Solving 15
Research and Research Summaries 16
Studies and Assessment 16
Computers and Technology 16

6 Calculus and Precalculus 17
School Mathematics 17
Precalculus 17
Elementary Calculus 17
Advanced Calculus 18
Supplementary Resources 18

7 Differential Equations 19
Introductory Texts 19
Advanced Topics 19

8 Analysis 20
Foundations of Analysis 20
Real Analysis 20
Fractals 20
Complex Analysis 21
Functional Analysis 21
Special Topics 21

9 Foundations and Mathematical Logic 21
Surveys 21
Logic 21
Set Theory 22
Model Theory 22

10 Discrete Mathematics 22
Discrete Mathematics 22
Finite Mathematics 22
Combinatorics 23
Graph Theory 23
Special Topics 24

11 Number Theory 24
    Introductory Texts 24
    Expositions 24
    Elementary Monographs 24
    Primes and Factors 25
    Algebraic Number Theory 25

12 Linear Algebra 25
    Elementary 25
    Advanced 25

13 Algebra 26
    Introductory Surveys 26
    Advanced Surveys 26
    Group Theory 26
    Rings and Ideals 26
    Fields and Galois Theory 27
    Commutative Algebra 27

14 Geometry 27
    General 27
    Surveys 27
    School Geometry 28
    Euclidean and Non-Euclidean Geometry . 28
    Polyhedra, Tilings, Symmetry 28
    Computational Geometry 28
    Algebraic and Differential Geometry .. 29
    Special Topics 29

15 Topology 29
    General Topology 29
    Geometric Topology 29
    Algebraic Topology 30
    Differential Topology 30

16 Vocational and Technical Mathematics .. 30
    Industrial Mathematics 30
    Mathematics for Trades 30
    Health Sciences 32
    Data Processing 32
    Electronics 32
    Chemical Technology 33
    Engineering Technology 33

17 Business Mathematics 34
    Basic Skills 34
    Algebra and Finite Mathematics 34
    Business Statistics 34

    Business Calculus 34
    Finance 35
    Management 35
    Actuarial Mathematics 35

18 Numerical Analysis 36
    Introductory Texts 36
    Advanced Topics 36
    Numerical Linear Algebra 36
    Approximation Theory 37
    Computer Methods 37

19 Modeling and Operations Research 37
    General 37
    Mathematical Modeling 37
    Game Theory 38
    Linear Programming 38
    Special Topics 38

20 Probability 39
    General 39
    Elementary 39
    Advanced 39
    Stochastic Processes 40
    Foundations 40
    Special Topics 40

21 Statistics 40
    General 40
    Introductory Texts 41
    Elementary 41
    Intermediate 41
    Data Analysis 42
    Linear Models and Regression Analysis .. 42
    Sampling and Survey Design 42
    Special Topics 42

22 Computer Science 43
    Computer Literacy 43
    Computers and Society 43
    Introductory 43
    Data Structures 44
    Database Systems 44
    Programming 44
    Programming Languages 44
    Algorithms 45
    Theory of Computation 45
    Software Systems 45
    Artificial Intelligence 45
    Software Engineering 46
    Compilers and Translators 46

Computer Graphics 46
Special Topics 46

23 Applications to Life Sciences 47

General 47
Ecology 47
Epidemiology 47
Genetics 47
Population Biology 48
Physiology 48

24 Applications to Physical Sciences 48

General 48
Introductory Texts 49

Advanced Surveys 49
Relativity 49
Cosmology and Celestial Mechanics 49
Information Theory 49

25 Applications to Social Sciences 50

General 50
Economics 50
Political Science 50
Psychology 51

26 Journals and Periodicals 51

Author Index 53

Preface

Strong libraries are of vital importance to an effective college environment in which students are expected to acquire the disposition for life-long learning. To accomplish this goal, colleges must develop curricula—in mathematics as in any other subject—that encourage students to learn to use a library. However, before that can happen, colleges must develop libraries worth using.

Unfortunately, college students rarely use library resources in their mathematical studies. Conventional curricula and common teaching practices rely almost exclusively on textbooks—despite substantial evidence that more engaging assignments based on richer resources lead to better understanding. Moreover, college libraries often have very thin and eccentric mathematics collections that are typically shaped more by happenstance than by careful planning that emphasizes balance of the collection as a whole. This process yields spotty collections that are often inadequate for either student or faculty needs.

Building a strong college library is much like building a strong curriculum. One must plan for the whole while ensuring balance of all the parts. In building libraries as in planning curricula, one must make tough choices. As not every good course can be taught, neither can every good book be purchased.

The current national imperative for revitalizing mathematics education adds a special sense of urgency to the need for balanced, contemporary undergraduate mathematics collections. A good library provides resources for students to broaden their mathematical horizons; opportunities for assignments that move beyond mere exercises to writing, reading, and exploration; and sources for faculty who are engaged in scholarship and curriculum development. Course-related library assignments are an essential bridge between textbook-based homework and career choices made during college years. Library improvement in the mathematical sciences is a necessary (but by no means sufficient) step along the path towards curriculum reform.

Background

Twenty-five years ago the Mathematical Association of America addressed a similar need by preparing *Basic Library Lists* for two-year and four-year colleges. The goal then was to encourage all colleges to build mathematics collections adequate to ensure that no student would be denied access to appropriate mathematical materials. Since these *Basic Library Lists* were last revised, over 15,000 books have been published in the mathematical sciences, many reflecting topics that have only recently become prominent.

Mathematics itself has undergone several major changes. Computers have emerged as a significant force in mathematics, introducing algorithmic thinking, discrete mathematics, data analysis, and mathematical logic as important and growing parts of the mathematical sciences. The increasing applicability of mathematics has created new demand for courses in mathematical modelling, in statistics, and in mathematical biology. The joining of applied mathematics with computing has created whole new disciplines on the periphery of mathematics, such as the theory of computation, simulation, scientific computation, and dynamical systems.

Powerful new methods of computational and applied mathematics have the potential to attract many good students to careers in mathematics. Unfortunately, these advances are often invisible to students at the early, formative stage of their college studies, since all they see in introductory courses are algebra, statistics, or calculus textbooks. Because of the long delay for modern topics to get into regular texts, it is very important that colleges be encouraged to develop instructional styles that introduce beginning students not only to textbooks, but also to library resources. For that to make educational sense, it is important that libraries use their limited budgets to build collections that will stimulate the interests of all prospective mathematics students, both those who might be attracted to major in a mathematical science as well as the many others who study mathematics for different purposes.

Objectives

Two-Year College Mathematics Library Recommendations contains approximately 1200 titles arranged in 25 chapters and 160 sections. Books have been selected according to several different objectives:

- To provide students with introductory material in various fields of the mathematical sciences that might not be part of their curriculum;
- To provide reading material that is collateral to regular courses;
- To extend the curriculum beyond regular course offerings;
- To provide faculty at two-year colleges with reference material that is relevant to their teaching and that will help broaden their mathematical expertise;
- To provide resources for independent study;
- To provide general readers with clear and lively exposition about the mathematical sciences and their applications;
- To ensure that two-year college libraries have important reference works and classic sources in the mathematical sciences;
- To provide students in disciplines that use the mathematical sciences with appropriate references.

To help libraries on limited budgets, books have been marked with asterisks to indicate priority:

     *** *Essential* (approximately 75 titles)
      ** *Highly recommended* (approximately 150 titles)
       * *Recommended* (approximately 300 titles)
        Listed (approximately 650 titles)

The final section contains recommendations for periodical and journal subscriptions in the mathematical sciences, marked in similar priority categories.

By its very nature, *Two-Year College Mathematics Library Recommendations* offers a comprehensive survey of the best literature in the mathematical sciences. Although intended primarily for libraries, the volume is also an excellent source of inspiration for self-study by anyone wishing to explore a new field or to catch up on the recent literature in a subject. The volume provides a truly panoramic window on the world of mathematics.

Procedures

This volume was prepared as part of a larger effort by a special subcommittee of the MAA's Committee on the Undergraduate Program in Mathematics (CUPM) to produce new editions of library lists for both two-year and four-year colleges. The new four-year list, *Library Recommendations for Undergraduate Mathematics*, contains approximately 3000 titles from which a special team of two-year college reviewers selected the 1200 that appear in the present volume.

Primary judgments for titles to be included in each chapter were provided by over 100 college and university mathematics faculty working in 25 teams according to subject area. Initial nominations were drawn from Telegraphic Reviews published in the *American Mathematical Monthly* and from the earlier *Basic Library List*. These initial nominations numbered in excess of 15,000 titles. After preliminary screening, titles were arranged by topic to provide 25 lists totaling approximately 4500 nominations to the discipline review teams. These teams then added another 1500 nominations before beginning the major task of establishing priorities.

The process of review has been long and detailed, requiring not only the melding of conflicting opinions by many different experts but also the checking of countless bibliographic details. The result is an amalgam of expert opinion, not a consensus of our many reviewers. Many judgments reflected in these *Recommendations* are shared by some reviewers but not by others. Our goal was not to make a list of "best books," but to produce a structured set of recommendations that would be useful to two-year college libraries, that would ensure balance by topic, and that would maintain reasonable limits on the number of recommendations.

Within these constraints, certain informal principles guided the many difficult choices that were required. Routine textbooks were given lower priority than other monographs because it is generally not wise for a library to devote scarce resources to ordinary student texts. In many subjects with dozens of comparable texts, we list a few titles to ensure coverage and omit many others that are essentially similar. In such cases our choices are not primarily a reflection of different quality but of desire to avoid needless duplication. We also tilted choices in favor of recent titles, since this is an area where library committees may be in greatest need of advice. Many old classics which are of great value, especially to libraries that already have them, are not included in our recommendations because new money would probably be more wisely spent on newer books.

Prudent use of these *Recommendations* requires judgment and dialogue between librarians and mathematicians. Many good and valuable books do not appear here, some being cut primarily to meet our self-imposed requirements of total length. Different libraries will view differently the relative priorities of textbooks, of references books, or of special monographs. In many situations, libraries may already have comparable books that are not on this list but that nevertheless provide important and equivalent coverage of certain areas. While the collection recommended here does constitute an excellent mathematics library for a two-year college, so would collections with other shapes and other titles. Limited library resources should be used not just to replicate this list as a whole, but to build strength in areas where coverage is thin.

Bibliographic Details

Mathematics is a multi-facted discipline with innumerable cross-linkages among widely separated specialties. These connections makes the subject fascinating even as they make the task of the bibliographer frustrating. Many titles could easily be listed in several different sections; some seem to fit no section at all. Notwithstanding the difficulties of logically neat classification, titles are listed only once, in some sub-area in which they seem to fit. No cross references have been used, since once begun such a task could go on almost without end.

Each title is listed with spare but adequate bibliographic detail, typically just author(s), title, publisher, and date. Other details such as translators, book series, or special editions are normally omitted. For books that have been revised or reprinted, we normally give only the most recent title with just two dates (and publishers): the first, and the most recent. We leave to librarians and their mathematics department advisors the subtle question of balancing the purchase of new editions against the purchase of new titles.

No attempt has been made to indicate whether books recommended here are still in print. Many are, and many are not. The thriving publication of reprints renders such information ephemeral, outdated before it would appear. Libraries interested in obtaining out-of-print titles can often secure them through used book markets. Perhaps the very presence of an old title among these *Recommendations* may cause some old classics to be reprinted.

The author index lists each author (or editor) named in the main bibliography together with title of the book and the section in which it appears. This allows anyone checking for particular titles to readily locate them in the main list, where full bibliographic details are provided.

Acknowledgements

Many people helped with this volume, some of whom I know only through the ubiquitous medium of e-mail. Twenty-five subject-area team leaders undertook the primary responsibility of organizing and amalgamating the diverse recommendations pertaining to each chapter of the bibliography. They were assisted by scores of reviewers who provided advice on various parts of the manuscript. Names of those who helped with various stages of the work are listed on the following pages. Everyone who may benefit from this volume owes these hard-working reviewers a real debt of gratitude.

Policy for the volume was set by a Steering Committee which was established by MAA as an *ad hoc* Subcommittee of CUPM. Advice from members of the Steering Committee was valuable at all stages of the process. I especially appreciated their counsel at key points where conflicting recommendations regarding policy needed to be resolved.

A special review committee for two-year colleges undertook the major task of selecting titles for this two-year college library volume. These individuals—Shelly Gordon, Peter Lindstrom, Glenn Miller, Sharon Ross—provided indispensable service in reviewing various drafts of this manuscript.

Typing and checking of innumerable bibliographic details was carried out with unfailing good humor over a period of more than two years by Mary Kay Peterson, who has also prepared every Telegraphic Review that has appeared in the *Monthly* for the last twenty years. This volume would never have been possible without the consistency provided by her careful attention to details, large and small.

Financial support for preparation of this long-overdue set of recommendations has been provided by grants from the National Science Foundation and the Exxon Education Foundation. Their support made it possible both to prepare the volume and to ensure its distribution to college libraries.

Despite numerous efforts to check and proof-read this set of recommendations, among the thousands of details there inevitably remain dozens of errors or inconsistencies—a missing edition here, a wrong date there. More substantial errors undoubtedly also occur, improperly categorized titles being the most likely. I hope that these occasional blemishes do not obscure the central purpose and value of the *Recommendations* as a whole: to provide two-year colleges with useful, contemporary guidance concerning the development of the mathematical sciences collections of their libraries.

Lynn Arthur Steen
St. Olaf College
November 1991

Steering Committee

DONALD J. ALBERS, Associate Director, Mathematical Association of America.

NANCY D. ANDERSON, Mathematics Librarian, University of Illinois, Urbana, IL.

PAUL J. CAMPBELL, Beloit College, Beloit, WI.

CHARLES R. HAMPTON, College of Wooster, Wooster, OH.

LYNN ARTHUR STEEN, St. Olaf College, Northfield, MN.

MARCIA P. SWARD, Executive Director, Mathematical Association of America.

ALAN C. TUCKER, SUNY at Stony Brook, Stony Brook, NY.

ANN E. WATKINS, California State University, Northridge, CA.

Two-Year College Review Team

SHELDON P. GORDON, Suffolk County Community College, Selden, NY.

PETER A. LINDSTROM, North Lake College, Irving, TX.

GLENN MILLER, Borough of Manhattan Community College, New York, NY.

SHARON CUTLER ROSS, DeKalb College, Clarkston, GA.

Team Leaders

GEORGE E. ANDREWS, Pennsylvania State University, University Park, PA. *(Number Theory)*

RON BARNES, University of Houston, Downtown, Houston, TX. *(Probability)*

JERRY L. BONA, Pennsylvania State University, University Park, PA. *(Physical Sciences)*

BARRY A. CIPRA, Northfield, MN. *(General)*

RAY E. COLLINGS, Tri-County Technical College, Pendleton, SC. *(Vocational Mathematics)*

R. STEPHEN CUNNINGHAM, California State University at Stanislaus, Turlock, CA. *(Computer Science)*

JOHN A. DOSSEY, Illinois State University, Normal, IL. *(Education)*

UNDERWOOD DUDLEY, DePauw University, Greencastle, IN. *(Recreational Mathematics)*

MEYER JERISON, Purdue University, West

Lafayette, IN. *(Analysis)*

BARBARA A. JUR, Macomb Community College, Warren, MI. *(Business Mathematics)*

GENEVIEVE M. KNIGHT, Coppin State College, Baltimore, MD. *(School Mathematics)*

SIMON A. LEVIN, Cornell University, Ithaca, NY. *(Life Sciences)*

R. BRUCE LIND, University of Puget Sound, Tacoma, WA. *(Statistics)*

DANIEL P. MAKI, Indiana University, Bloomington, IN. *(Operations Research)*

JOSEPH MALKEVITCH, York College of CUNY, Jamaica, NY. *(Geometry)*

WALTER E. MIENTKA, University of Nebraska, Lincoln, NE. *(High School Libraries)*

KENNETH C. MILLETT, University of California, Santa Barbara, CA. *(Topology)*

HAL G. MOORE, Brigham Young University, Provo, UT. *(Algebra)*

YVES NIEVERGELT, Eastern Washington University, Cheney, WA. *(Numerical Analysis)*

INGRAM OLKIN, Stanford University, Stanford, CA. *(Social Sciences)*

VERA PLESS, University of Illinois at Chicago, Chicago, IL. *(Discrete Mathematics)*

MARIAN POUR-EL, University of Minnesota, Minneapolis, MN. *(Foundations)*

SAMUEL M. RANKIN III, Worcester Polytech-nic Institute, Worcester, MA. *(Differential Equations)*

FREDERICK RICKEY, Bowling Green State University, Bowling Green, OH. *(History)*

JIMMY L. SOLOMON, Mississippi State University, Mississippi State, MS. *(Linear Algebra)*

ALVIN SWIMMER, Arizona State University, Tempe, AZ. *(Calculus)*

Reviewers

JOE ALBREE, Auburn University at Montgomery, Montgomery, AL.

RICHARD ASKEY, University of Wisconsin, Madison, WI.

ED BENDER, J. Sargeant Reynolds Community College, Richmond, VA.

BRUCE C. BERNDT, University of Illinois, Urbana, IL.

WILLIAM D. BLAIR, Northern Illinois University, DeKalb, IL.

WILLIAM E. BOYCE, Rensselaer Polytechnic Institute, Troy, NY.

ANNE E. BROWN, Saint Mary's College, Notre Dame, IN.

GARY BROWN, College of St. Benedict, St. Joseph, MN.

BARRY BRUNSON, Western Kentucky University, Bowling Green, KY.

JOE P. BUHLER, Reed College, Portland, OR.

DONALD BUSHAW, Washington State University, Pullman, WA.

THOMAS J. CARTER, California State University at Stanislaus, Turlock, CA.

J. KEVIN COLLIGAN, National Security Agency, Fort Meade, MD.

MIRIAM P. COONEY, Saint Mary's College, Notre Dame, IN.

ELLIS CUMBERBATCH, Claremont Graduate School, Claremont, CA.

JOHN DAUGHTRY, East Carolina University, Greenville, NC.

NATHANIEL DEAN, Bell Communications Research, Morristown, NJ.

KEITH DEVLIN, Colby College, Waterville, ME.

MARJORIE ENNEKING, Portland State University, Portland, OR.

MARCUS W. FELDMAN, Stanford University, Stanford, CA.

J. CHRIS FISHER, University of Regina, Regina, Saskatchewan, Canada.

BEN A. FUSARO, Salisbury State University, Salisbury, MD.

STEVE GALOVICH, Carleton College, Northfield, MN.

ALAN J. GOLDMAN, Johns Hopkins University, Baltimore, MD.

RONALD J. GOULD, Emory University, Atlanta, GA.

SANDY GRABINER, Pomona College, Claremont, CA.

PAUL R. HALMOS, Santa Clara University, Santa Clara, CA.

JAMES L. HARTMAN, College of Wooster, Wooster, OH.

BRYAN HEARSEY, Lebanon Valley College, Annville, PA.

M. KATHLEEN HEID, Pennsylvania State University, University Park, PA.

ISOM HERRON, Howard University, Washington, DC.

LINDA HILL, Idaho State University, Pocatello, ID.

PAT HIRSCHY, Delaware Technical and Community College, Wilmington, DE.

FREDERICK HOFFMAN, Florida Atlantic University, Boca Raton, FL.

MARY ANN HOVIS, Lima Technical College, Lima, OH.

THOMAS W. HUNGERFORD, Cleveland State University, Cleveland, OH.

ELEANOR GREEN JONES, Norfolk State University, Norfolk, VA.

ROBERT E. KENNEDY, Central Missouri State University, Warrensburg, MO.

MARTHA J. KIRKER, Iowa State University, Ames, IA.

SHANTHA KRISHNAMACHARI, Borough of Manhattan Community College, New York, NY.

DONALD KRUG, Northern Kentucky University, Highland Heights, KY.

CAROL W. KUBLIN, SUNY College of Agriculture and Technology, Cobleskill, NY.

STEPHEN KUHN, University of Tennessee at Chattanooga, Chattanooga, TN.

JAMES M. LANDWEHR, AT&T Bell Labs, Murray Hill, NJ.

ANTHONY LOBELLO, Allegheny College, Meadville, PA.

WILLIAM LUCAS, Claremont Graduate School, Claremont, CA.

MICHAEL MCASEY, Bradley University, Peoria, IL.

DUSA MCDUFF, SUNY at Stony Brook, Stony Brook, NY.

ROGERS J. NEWMAN, Southern University, Baton Rouge, LA.

ARNOLD OSTEBEE, St. Olaf College, Northfield, MN.

PETER PAPPAS, Vassar College, Poughkeepsie, NY.

MARY R. PARKER, Austin Community College, Austin, TX.

WALTER M. PATTERSON III, Lander College, Greenwood, SC.

MEE SEE PHUA, University of the District of Columbia, Washington, DC.

JAMES D. REID, Wesleyan University, Middletown, CT.

ROBERT O. ROBSON, Oregon State University, Corvallis, OR.

THOMAS A. ROMBERG, University of Wisconsin, Madison, WI.

FRANCES ROSAMOND, National University, San Diego, CA.

PETER ROSS, Santa Clara University, Santa Clara, CA.

JAMES L. ROVNYAK, University of Virginia, Charlottesville, VA.

RICHARD L. SCHEAFFER, University of Florida, Gainesville, FL.

JOHN SCHUE, Macalester College, St. Paul, MN.

RAE MICHAEL SHORTT, Wesleyan University, Middletown, CT.

TOM SIBLEY, St. John's University, Collegeville, MN.

MARTHA J. SIEGEL, Towson State University, Towson, MD.

STEPHANIE SLOYAN, Georgian Court College, Lakewood, NJ.

CARL R. SPITZNAGEL, John Carroll University, Cleveland, OH.

ELIZABETH J. TELES, Montgomery College, Takoma Park, MD.

ALLEN TUCKER, Bowdoin College, Brunswick, ME.

THOMAS TUCKER, Colgate University, Hamilton, NY.

WILLIAM C. WATERHOUSE, Penn State University, University Park, PA.

JOAN WYZKOSKI WEISS, Fairfield University, Fairfield, CT.

JULIAN WEISSGLASS, Mathematical Sciences Education Board, Washington, DC.

CAROL WOOD, Wesleyan University, Middletown, CT.

1 General

1.1 General Anthologies

** ALEKSANDROV, A.D.; KOLMOGOROV, ANDREI N.; AND LAVRENT'EV, M.A., EDS. *Mathematics: Its Content, Methods, and Meaning*, 3 Vols. Cambridge, MA: MIT Press, 1969.

BEHNKE, H., *et al.*, EDS. *Fundamentals of Mathematics*, 3 Vols. Cambridge, MA: MIT Press, 1974, 1983.

BOEHM, GEORGE A.W. *The Mathematical Sciences: A Collection of Essays.* Cambridge, MA: MIT Press, 1969.

CAMPBELL, DOUGLAS M. AND HIGGINS, JOHN C., EDS. *Mathematics: People, Problems, Results,* 3 Vols. Belmont, CA: Wadsworth, 1984.

*** NEWMAN, JAMES R. *The World of Mathematics,* 4 Vols. New York, NY: Simon and Schuster, 1956; Redmond, WA: Microsoft Press, 1988.

* SCIENTIFIC AMERICAN. *Mathematics in the Modern World.* New York, NY: W.H. Freeman, 1968.

** STEEN, LYNN ARTHUR, ED. *Mathematics Today: Twelve Informal Essays.* New York, NY: Springer-Verlag, 1978, 1984.

* STEEN, LYNN ARTHUR, ED. *Mathematics Tomorrow.* New York, NY: Springer-Verlag, 1981.

1.2 Elementary Exposition

ASIMOV, ISAAC. *Asimov on Numbers.* New York, NY: Doubleday, 1977.

BELL, ERIC T. *Mathematics: Queen and Servant of Science.* Washington, DC: Mathematical Association of America, 1987.

BUNCH, BRYAN H. *Mathematical Fallacies and Paradoxes.* New York, NY: Van Nostrand Reinhold, 1982.

** COURANT, RICHARD AND ROBBINS, H. *What is Mathematics?* New York, NY: Oxford University Press, 1941.

DANTZIG, TOBIAS. *Number, The Language of Science,* Fourth Edition. New York, NY: Free Press, 1967.

* DAVIS, PHILIP J. AND HERSH, REUBEN. *Descartes' Dream: The World According to Mathematics.* San Diego, CA: Harcourt Brace Jovanovich, 1986; New York, NY: Penguin, 1988.

* DAVIS, PHILIP J. AND HERSH, REUBEN. *The Mathematical Experience.* New York, NY: Birkhäuser, 1980.

DEVLIN, KEITH J. *Mathematics: The New Golden Age.* New York, NY: Penguin, 1988.

GÅRDING, LARS. *Encounter with Mathematics.* New York, NY: Springer-Verlag, 1977.

*** GLEICK, JAMES. *Chaos: Making a New Science.* New York, NY: Viking Press, 1987.

GUILLEN, MICHAEL. *Bridges to Infinity: The Human Side of Mathematics.* Boston, MA: Houghton Mifflin, 1983.

*** HARDY, G.H. *A Mathematician's Apology,* Revised Edition. New York, NY: Cambridge University Press, 1967, 1969.

HOFFMAN, PAUL. *Archimedes' Revenge: The Joys and Perils of Mathematics.* New York, NY: W.W. Norton, 1988.

* HOFSTADTER, DOUGLAS R. *Gödel, Escher, Bach: An Eternal Golden Braid.* New York, NY: Basic Books, 1979.

HOFSTADTER, DOUGLAS R. *Metamagical Themas: Questing for the Essence of Mind and Pattern.* New York, NY: Basic Books, 1985.

* HONSBERGER, ROSS. *Ingenuity in Mathematics.* Washington, DC: Mathematical Association of America, 1975.

* HONSBERGER, ROSS. *Mathematical Gems,* 3 Vols. Washington, DC: Mathematical Association of America, 1973–85.

* HONSBERGER, ROSS. *Mathematical Morsels.* Washington, DC: Mathematical Association of America, 1978.

* HONSBERGER, ROSS. *Mathematical Plums.* Washington, DC: Mathematical Association of America, 1979.

* HONSBERGER, ROSS. *More Mathematical Morsels.* Washington, DC: Mathematical Association of America, 1991.

** KAPPRAFF, JAY. *Connections: The Geometric Bridge Between Art and Science.* New York, NY: McGraw-Hill, 1991.

KLINE, MORRIS. *Mathematics and the Search for Knowledge.* New York, NY: Oxford University Press, 1985.

KLINE, MORRIS. *Mathematics: The Loss of Certainty.* New York, NY: Oxford University Press, 1980.

** MORRISON, PHILIP AND MORRISON, PHYLIS. *Powers of Ten.* New York, NY: W.H. Freeman, 1982.

*** NIVEN, IVAN M. *Maxima and Minima Without Calculus.* Washington, DC: Mathematical Association of America, 1981.

* PAULOS, JOHN ALLEN. *Beyond Numeracy: Ruminations of a Numbers Man.* New York, NY: Alfred A. Knopf, 1991.

PAULOS, JOHN ALLEN. *Innumeracy: Mathematical Illiteracy and Its Consequences.* New York, NY: Hill and Wang, 1988.

PEDOE, DAN. *The Gentle Art of Mathematics.* New York, NY: Macmillan, 1963.

PENROSE, ROGER. *The Emperor's New Mind: Concerning Computers, Minds, and The Laws of Physics.* New York, NY: Oxford University Press, 1989.

** PETERSON, IVARS. *Islands of Truth.* New York, NY: W.H. Freeman, 1991.

** PETERSON, IVARS. *The Mathematical Tourist: Snapshots of Modern Mathematics.* New York, NY: W.H. Freeman, 1988.

RADEMACHER, HANS AND TOEPLITZ, OTTO. *The Enjoyment of Mathematics.* Princeton, NJ: Princeton University Press, 1957.

** RADEMACHER, HANS. *Higher Mathematics from an Elementary Point of View.* New York, NY: Birkhäuser, 1983.

SCHOENBERG, I.J. *Mathematical Time Exposures.* Washington, DC: Mathematical Association of America, 1982.

STEINHAUS, HUGO. *Mathematical Snapshots,* Third Edition. New York, NY: Oxford University Press, 1969, 1983.

* STEWART, IAN. *Concepts of Modern Mathematics.* New York, NY: Penguin, 1975.

* STEWART, IAN. *Does God Play Dice? The Mathematics of Chaos.* New York, NY: Penguin, 1989.

* STEWART, IAN. *The Problems of Mathematics.* New York, NY: Oxford University Press, 1987.

WHITEHEAD, ALFRED NORTH. *An Introduction to Mathematics.* New York, NY: Oxford University Press, 1958.

1.3 Advanced Surveys

* BOCHNER, SALOMON. *The Role of Mathematics in the Rise of Science.* Princeton, NJ: Princeton University Press, 1981.

DÖRRIE, HEINRICH. *100 Great Problems of Elementary Mathematics.* Mineola, NY: Dover, 1965.

KAC, MARK; ROTA, GIAN-CARLO; AND SCHWARTZ, JACOB T. *Discrete Thoughts: Essays on Mathematics, Science, and Philosophy.* New York, NY: Birkhäuser, 1986.

SAWYER, W.W. *Introducing Mathematics,* 4 Vols. New York, NY: Penguin, 1964–70.

SCHIFFER, M.M. AND BOWDEN, LEON. *The Role of Mathematics in Science.* Washington, DC: Mathematical Association of America, 1984.

* TIETZE, HEINRICH. *Famous Problems of Mathematics: Solved and Unsolved Mathematical Problems From Antiquity to Modern Times.* Baltimore, MD: Graylock Press, 1965.

1.4 Mathematics Appreciation Texts

** CONSORTIUM FOR MATHEMATICS AND ITS APPLICATIONS. *For All Practical Purposes: Introduction to Contemporary Mathematics,* Second Edition. New York, NY: W.H. Freeman, 1988, 1991.

*** DUNHAM, WILLIAM. *Journey Through Genius: The Great Theorems of Mathematics.* New York, NY: John Wiley, 1990.

** GARDINER, A. *Discovering Mathematics: The Art of Investigation.* New York, NY: Oxford University Press, 1987.

GOLOS, ELLERY B. *Patterns in Mathematics.* Boston, MA: Prindle, Weber and Schmidt, 1981.

GOWAR, NORMAN. *An Invitation to Mathematics.* New York, NY: Oxford University Press, 1979.

HERSTEIN, I.N. AND KAPLANSKY, IRVING. *Matters Mathematical,* Second Edition. New York, NY: Harper and Row, 1974; New York, NY: Chelsea, 1978.

* JACOBS, HAROLD R. *Mathematics: A Human Endeavor,* Second Edition. New York, NY: W.H. Freeman, 1970, 1982.

MILLER, CHARLES D.; HEEREN, VERN E.; AND HORNSBY, E. JOHN, JR. *Mathematical Ideas,* Sixth Edition. Glenview, IL: Scott Foresman, 1970, 1990.

ROBERTS, A. WAYNE AND VARBERG, DALE E. *Faces of Mathematics: An Introductory Course for College Students,* Second Edition. New York, NY: Thomas Y. Crowell, 1978; New York, NY: Harper and Row, 1982.

SMITH, KARL J. *Mathematics, Its Power and Utility,* Third Edition. Pacific Grove, CA: Brooks/Cole, 1983, 1989.

SMITH, KARL J. *The Nature of Mathematics,* Sixth Edition. Pacific Grove, CA: Brooks/Cole, 1991.

STEIN, SHERMAN K. *Mathematics, The Man-made Universe: An Introduction to the Spirit of Mathematics,* Third Edition. New York, NY: W.H. Freeman, 1976.

1.5 Fiction, Aphorisms, Epigrams

*** ABBOTT, EDWIN A. *Flatland.* Mineola, NY: Dover, 1952; Princeton, NJ: Princeton University Press, 1991.

* DEWDNEY, A.K. *The Planiverse.* New York, NY: Poseidon Press, 1984.

* EVES, HOWARD W. *Mathematical Circles,* Six Volume Series (Various Titles). Boston, MA: Prindle, Weber and Schmidt, 1969–88.

FADIMAN, CLIFTON. *Fantasia Mathematica.* New York, NY: Simon and Schuster, 1958.

FADIMAN, CLIFTON. *The Mathematical Magpie.* New York, NY: Simon and Schuster, 1962.

KNUTH, DONALD E. *Surreal Numbers.* Reading, MA: Addison-Wesley, 1974.

1.6 Miscellany

DAVIS, PHILIP J. AND CHINN, WILLIAM G. *3.1416 And All That.* New York, NY: Birkhäuser, 1985.

FOMENKO, ANATOLĬ T. *Mathematical Impressions.* Providence, RI: American Mathematical Society, 1990.

* HUNTLEY, H.E. *The Divine Proportion: A Study in Mathematical Beauty.* Mineola, NY: Dover, 1970.

** LANG, SERGE. *The Beauty of Doing Mathematics: Three Public Dialogues.* New York, NY: Springer-Verlag, 1985.

** PAGE, WARREN, ED. *Two-Year College Mathematics Readings.* Washington, DC: Mathematical Association of America, 1981.

2 Reference

2.1 Dictionaries

* DAINTITH, JOHN AND NELSON, R.D., EDS. *The Penguin Dictionary of Mathematics.* New York, NY: Penguin, 1989.

HOWSON, A. GEOFFREY. *A Handbook of Terms Used in Algebra and Analysis.* New York, NY: Cambridge University Press, 1972.

** JAMES, GLENN AND JAMES, ROBERT C., EDS. *Mathematical Dictionary,* Fourth Edition. New York, NY: Van Nostrand Reinhold, 1976.

SNEDDON, I.N., ED. *Encyclopedic Dictionary of Mathematics for Engineers and Applied Scientists.* Elmsford, NY: Pergamon Press, 1976.

TIETJEN, GARY L. *A Topical Dictionary of Statistics.* New York, NY: Chapman and Hall, 1986.

2.2 Handbooks

*** BEYER, WILLIAM H., ED. *CRC Handbook of Mathematical Sciences,* Sixth Edition. Boca Raton, FL: CRC Press, 1987.

* BEYER, WILLIAM H., ED. *CRC Standard Mathematical Tables and Formulas,* 29th Edition. Boca Raton, FL: CRC Press, 1991. *Ref QA47 M315 1987*

* BORWEIN, JONATHAN M. AND BORWEIN, PETER B. *A Dictionary of Real Numbers.* Belmont, CA: Wadsworth, 1990.

* BRONSHTEIN, I.N. AND SEMENDYAYEV, K.A. *Handbook of Mathematics.* New York, NY: Van Nostrand Reinhold, 1985.

BURINGTON, RICHARD S. AND MAY, DONALD C., JR. *Handbook of Probability and Statistics with Tables,* Second Edition. New York, NY: McGraw-Hill, 1970.

JOLLEY, L.B.W. *Summation of Series,* Second Revised Edition. Mineola, NY: Dover, 1961.

LAWRENCE, J. DENNIS. *A Catalog of Special Plane Curves.* Mineola, NY: Dover, 1972.

* SLOANE, N.J.A. *A Handbook of Integer Sequences.* New York, NY: Academic Press, 1973.

SPANIER, JEROME AND OLDHAM, KEITH B. *An Atlas of Functions.* New York, NY: Hemisphere, 1987.

VON SEGGERN, DAVID H. *CRC Handbook of Mathematical Curves and Surfaces.* Boca Raton, FL: CRC Press, 1990.

2.3 Encyclopedias

** AMERICAN COUNCIL OF LEARNED SOCIETIES. *Biographical Dictionary of Mathematicians.* New York, NY: Charles Scribner's, 1991.

*** GELLERT, WALTER, *et al.,* EDS. *The VNR Concise Encyclopedia of Mathematics.* New York, NY: Van Nostrand Reinhold, 1975.

* GILLISPIE, CHARLES C., ED. *Dictionary of Scientific Biography,* 16 Vols. plus Suppl. New York, NY: Charles Scribner's, 1970–90. *Ref Q141 D5*

* IYANAGA, SHÔKICHI AND KAWADA, YUKIYOSI, EDS. *Encyclopedic Dictionary of Mathematics.* Cambridge, MA: MIT Press, 1977, 1986.

** KOTZ, SAMUEL AND JOHNSON, NORMAN L., EDS. *Encyclopedia of Statistical Sciences.* New York, NY: John Wiley, 1982–88.

2.4 Bibliographies

* DAUBEN, JOSEPH W. *The History of Mathematics from Antiquity to the Present: A Selective Bibliography.* New York, NY: Garland, 1985.

** GAFFNEY, MATTHEW P. AND STEEN, LYNN ARTHUR. *Annotated Bibliography of Expository Writing in the Mathematical Sciences.* Washington, DC: Mathematical Association of America, 1976.

MAY, KENNETH O. *Bibliography and Research Manual of the History of Mathematics.* Toronto: University of Toronto Press, 1973.

* SCHAAF, WILLIAM L. *A Bibliography of Recreational Mathematics,* 4 Vols. Reston, VA: National Council of Teachers of Mathematics, 1955–78.

SCHAAF, WILLIAM L. *Mathematics and Science: An Adventure in Postage Stamps.* Reston, VA: National Council of Teachers of Mathematics, 1978.

SCHAEFER, BARBARA K. *Using the Mathematical Literature: A Practical Guide.* New York, NY: Marcel Dekker, 1979.

2.5 Indexes

MAY, KENNETH O. *Index of the American Mathematical Monthly, Volumes 1–80 (1894–1973).* Washington, DC: Mathematical Association of America, 1977.

NATIONAL COUNCIL OF TEACHERS OF MATHEMATICS. *Cumulative Index, The Arithmetic Teacher: 1974–1983,* Vols. 21–30. Reston, VA: National Council of Teachers of Mathematics, 1984.

* NATIONAL COUNCIL OF TEACHERS OF MATHEMATICS. *The Mathematics Teacher: Cumulative Indices,* Vols 1–68, 59–68, 69–78; 1908–65, 1966–75, 1976–85. Reston, VA: National Council of Teachers of Mathematics, 1967, 1976, 1988.

* SEEBACH, J. ARTHUR, JR. AND STEEN, LYNN ARTHUR, EDS. *Mathematics Magazine: 50 Year Index.* Washington, DC: Mathematical Association of America, 1978.

3 History

3.1 Surveys

*** BOYER, CARL B. AND MERZBACH, UTA C. *A History of Mathematics,* Second Edition. Princeton, NJ: Princeton University Press, 1985; New York, NY: John Wiley, 1968, 1991. *lost*

BURTON, DAVID M. *The History of Mathematics: An Introduction,* Second Edition. Needham Heights, MA: Allyn and Bacon, 1985; Dubuque, IA: William C. Brown, 1991.

** CAJORI, FLORIAN. *A History of Mathematical Notations.* Peru, IL: Open Court, 1974.

CAJORI, FLORIAN. *A History of Mathematics,* Fifth Edition. New York, NY: Chelsea, 1980, 1991. *3rd ed. 있음 c나*

COOLIDGE, JULIAN L. *The Mathematics of Great Amateurs,* Second Edition. New York, NY: Oxford University Press, 1949, 1990.

DIEUDONNÉ, JEAN. *Abrégé d'histoire des Mathématiques, 1700–1900,* 2 Vols. Paris: Hermann, 1978.

*** EVES, HOWARD W. *An Introduction to the History of Mathematics with Cultural Connections,* Sixth Edition. New York, NY: Rinehart and Co., 1953; Philadelphia, PA: Saunders College, 1990.

** FAUVEL, JOHN AND GRAY, JEREMY, EDS. *The History of Mathematics: A Reader.* London: Macmillan Press and Open University, 1987.

HOLLINGDALE, STUART. *Makers of Mathematics.* New York, NY: Penguin, 1989.

KLINE, MORRIS. *Mathematical Thought from Ancient to Modern Times.* New York, NY: Oxford University Press, 1972.

KLINE, MORRIS. *Mathematics in Western Culture.* New York, NY: Oxford University Press, 1953, 1971.

** KRAMER, EDNA E. *The Nature and Growth of Modern Mathematics.* New York, NY: Fawcett World Library, 1974; Princeton, NJ: Princeton University Press, 1982.

PHILLIPS, ESTHER R., ED. *Studies in the History of Mathematics.* Washington, DC: Mathematical Association of America, 1987.

ROWE, DAVID E. AND MCCLEARY, JOHN, EDS. *The History of Modern Mathematics,* 2 Vols. New York, NY: Academic Press, 1989.

* SMITH, DAVID EUGENE. *History of Mathematics,* 2 Vols. New York, NY: Ginn and Co., 1923; Mineola, NY: Dover, 1958.

STILLWELL, JOHN. *Mathematics and Its History.* New York, NY: Springer-Verlag, 1989.

* STRUIK, DIRK JAN. *A Concise History of Mathematics,* Fourth Revised Edition. Mineola, NY: Dover, 1987.

3.2 Biographies

AITON, E.J. *Leibniz: A Biography.* New York, NY: Adam Hilger, 1985.

✓ *** ALBERS, DONALD J. AND ALEXANDERSON, GERALD L., EDS. *Mathematical People: Profiles and Interviews.* New York, NY: Birkhäuser, 1985. *Ref QA 28 W37 1985*

✓ *** ALBERS, DONALD J., et al., EDS. *More Mathematical People.* New York, NY: Academic Press, 1990. *Ref QA 28 M67 1990*

BAUM, JOAN. *The Calculating Passion of Ada Byron.* Hamden, CT: Archon Books, 1986.

* BEDINI, SILVIO. *The Life of Benjamin Banneker.* New York, NY: Charles Scribner's, 1972.

BELL, ERIC T. *Men of Mathematics.* New York, NY: Simon and Schuster, 1937.

BOX, JOAN FISHER. *R.A. Fisher: The Life of a Scientist.* New York, NY: John Wiley, 1978.

BREWER, JAMES W. AND SMITH, MARTHA K., EDS. *Emmy Noether: A Tribute to Her Life and Work.* New York, NY: Marcel Dekker, 1981.

** BÜHLER, WALTER K. *Gauss: A Biographical Study.* New York, NY: Springer-Verlag, 1981.

BURKS, ALICE R. AND BURKS, ARTHUR W. *The First Electronic Computer: The Atanasoff Story.* Ann Arbor, MI: University of Michigan Press, 1988.

COOPER, NECIA G., ED. *From Cardinals to Chaos: Reflections on the Life and Legacy of Stanislaw Ulam.* New York, NY: Cambridge University Press, 1989.

DAUBEN, JOSEPH W. *Georg Cantor: His Mathematics and Philosophy of the Infinite.* Cambridge, MA: Harvard University Press, 1979; Princeton, NJ: Princeton University Press, 1990.

* DICK, AUGUSTE. *Emmy Noether, 1882–1935.* New York, NY: Birkhäuser, 1981.

* HALMOS, PAUL R. *I Want To Be A Mathematician: An Automathography in Three Parts.* Washington, DC: Mathematical Association of America, 1985; New York, NY: Springer-Verlag, 1985.

* HARDY, G.H. *Ramanujan,* Third Edition. New York, NY: Chelsea, 1960, 1968.

** HODGES, ANDREW. *Alan Turing, The Enigma.* New York, NY: Simon and Schuster, 1983.

* HOFFMANN, BANESH. *Albert Einstein: Creator and Rebel.* New York, NY: Viking Press, 1972.

* INFELD, LEOPOLD. *Whom the Gods Love: The Story of Evariste Galois.* Reston, VA: National Council of Teachers of Mathematics, 1978.

✓ *** KANIGEL, ROBERT. *The Man Who Knew Infinity: A Life of the Indian Genius Ramanujan.* New York, NY: Charles Scribner's, 1991. *QA 29 R3 K36 1991*

KOBLITZ, ANN HIBNER. *A Convergence of Lives, Sofia Kovalevskaia: Scientist, Writer, Revolutionary.* New York, NY: Birkhäuser, 1983.

* MACHALE, DESMOND. *George Boole: His Life and Work.* Dublin: Boole Press, 1985.

ORE, OYSTEIN. *Cardano: The Gambling Scholar.* Princeton, NJ: Princeton University Press, 1953; Mineola, NY: Dover, 1965.

ORE, OYSTEIN. *Niels Henrik Abel: Mathematician Extraordinary.* Minneapolis, MN: University of Minnesota Press, 1957; New York, NY: Chelsea, 1974.

** REID, CONSTANCE. *Hilbert.* (Combined edition, *Hilbert-Courant.*) New York, NY: Springer-Verlag, 1970, 1986.

RUSSELL, BERTRAND. *The Autobiography of Bertrand Russell,* 2 Vols. New York, NY: Simon and Schuster, 1968, 1969.

** ULAM, S.M. *Adventures of a Mathematician.* New York, NY: Charles Scribner's, 1976.

** WESTFALL, RICHARD S. *Never at Rest: A Biography of Isaac Newton.* New York, NY: Cambridge University Press, 1983.

WIENER, NORBERT. *Ex-Prodigy: My Childhood and Youth* and *I Am A Mathematician: Life of a Prodigy.* Cambridge, MA: MIT Press, 1953, 1956.

3.3 Source Books

CALINGER, RONALD, ED. *Classics of Mathematics*. Oak Park, IL: Moore, 1982.

** SMITH, DAVID EUGENE. *A Source Book in Mathematics*. New York, NY: McGraw-Hill, 1929; Mineola, NY: Dover, 1959.

STRUIK, DIRK JAN, ED. *A Source Book in Mathematics, 1200–1800*. Cambridge, MA: Harvard University Press, 1969; Princeton, NJ: Princeton University Press, 1986. QA21 S88

3.4 Classic Works

BERNDT, BRUCE C. *Ramanujan's Notebooks*, Parts I-III. New York, NY: Springer-Verlag, 1985–91.

* BOOLE, GEORGE. *Treatise on the Calculus of Finite Differences*, Fifth Edition. New York, NY: Chelsea, 1958.

* CARDANO, GIROLAMO. *The Great Art or the Rules of Algebra*. Cambridge, MA: MIT Press, 1968.

* CHACE, ARNOLD B. *The Rhind Mathematical Papyrus*. Reston, VA: National Council of Teachers of Mathematics, 1979.

CHRYSTAL, GEORGE. *Textbook of Algebra*, 2 Vols., Seventh Edition. New York, NY: Chelsea, 1964.

* DEDEKIND, RICHARD. *Essays on the Theory of Numbers*. Mineola, NY: Dover, 1963.

** DIJKSTERHUIS, E.J. *Archimedes*. Princeton, NJ: Princeton University Press, 1987.

EULER, LEONHARD. *Introduction to Analysis of the Infinite*, 2 Vols. New York, NY: Springer-Verlag, 1988, 1990.

* GALILEI, GALILEO. *Dialogues Concerning Two New Sciences*. Mineola, NY: Dover, 1954.

HALSTED, GEORGE B., ED. *Girolamo Saccheri's Euclides Vindicatus*. New York, NY: Chelsea, 1986.

HEATH, THOMAS L., ED. *The Works of Archimedes*. New York, NY: Cambridge University Press, 1897; Mineola, NY: Dover, 1953, 1964.

HEATH, THOMAS L. *Apollonius of Perga*. Cambridge: W. Haffer, 1986.

HEATH, THOMAS L. *Aristarchus of Samos: The Ancient Copernicus*. Oxford: Clarendon Press, 1913; Mineola, NY: Dover, 1981.

HEATH, THOMAS L. *Diophantus of Alexandria*. Cambridge: Cambridge University Press, 1885; Mineola, NY: Dover, 1964.

** HEATH, THOMAS L. *The Thirteen Books of Euclid's Elements*, 3 Vols. Mineola, NY: Dover, 1956.

LAM, LAY YONG. *A Critical Study of the Yang Hui Suan Fa: A Thirteenth-century Chinese Mathematical Treatise*. Singapore: Singapore University Press, 1977.

* SIGLER, L.E. *Leonardo Pisano Fibonacci: The Book of Squares*. New York, NY: Academic Press, 1987.

* SMITH, DAVID EUGENE AND LATHAM, MARCIA L. *The Geometry of René Descartes*. Mineola, NY: Dover, 1954.

SWETZ, FRANK J. *Capitalism and Arithmetic: The New Math of the 15th Century*, incl. *Treviso Arithmetic* (1487). La Salle, IL: Open Court, 1987.

VIÈTE, FRANÇOIS. *The Analytic Art*. Kent, OH: Kent State University Press, 1983.

WHITESIDE, D.T., ED. *The Mathematical Papers of Isaac Newton*, 8 Vols. New York, NY: Cambridge University Press, 1967–81.

3.5 Ancient and Medieval

** AABOE, ASGER. *Episodes from the Early History of Mathematics*. Washington, DC: Mathematical Association of America, 1964.

* BERGGREN, J.L. *Episodes in the Mathematics of Medieval Islam*. New York, NY: Springer-Verlag, 1986.

* EDWARDS, A.W.F. *Pascal's Arithmetical Triangle*. New York, NY: Oxford University Press, 1987.

* EVES, HOWARD W. *Great Moments in Mathematics (Before 1650)*. Washington, DC: Mathematical Association of America, 1980.

GILLINGS, RICHARD J. *Mathematics in the Times of the Pharaohs*. Mineola, NY: Dover, 1982.

** HEATH, THOMAS L. *A History of Greek Mathematics*, 2 Vols. Mineola, NY: Dover, 1981.

KLEIN, JACOB. *Greek Mathematical Thought and the Origin of Algebra.* Cambridge, MA: MIT Press, 1968.

LĪ YĂN AND DÙ SHÍRÁN. *Chinese Mathematics: A Concise History.* New York, NY: Clarendon Press, 1987.

NEUGEBAUER, O. *The Exact Sciences in Antiquity,* Second Edition. Providence, RI: Brown University Press, 1970.

SWETZ, FRANK J. AND KAO, T.I. *Was Pythagoras Chinese? An Examination of Right Triangle Theory in Ancient China.* Reston, VA: National Council of Teachers of Mathematics, 1977.

VAN DER WAERDEN, B.L. *Geometry and Algebra in Ancient Civilizations.* New York, NY: Springer-Verlag, 1983.

* VAN DER WAERDEN, B.L. *Science Awakening,* 2 Vols. Groningen: Wolters-Noordhoff, 1954; New York, NY: Oxford University Press, 1961; Princeton Junction, NJ: Scholar's Bookshelf, 1988.

** WILDER, RAYMOND L. *Evolution of Mathematical Concepts: An Elementary Study.* New York, NY: John Wiley, 1968; New York, NY: Halsted Press, 1973.

3.6 Modern

ALBERS, DONALD J.; ALEXANDERSON, GERALD L.; AND REID, CONSTANCE. *International Mathematical Congresses: An Illustrated History, 1893–1986.* New York, NY: Springer-Verlag, 1987.

DAUBEN, JOSEPH W., ED. *Mathematical Perspectives: Essays on Mathematics and Its Historical Development.* New York, NY: Academic Press, 1981.

* DUREN, PETER; ASKEY, RICHARD A.; AND MERZBACH, UTA C., EDS. *A Century of Mathematics in America,* 3 Vols. Providence, RI: American Mathematical Society, 1988–1989.

* EVES, HOWARD W. *Great Moments in Mathematics (After 1650).* Washington, DC: Mathematical Association of America, 1981.

HALMOS, PAUL R. *I Have A Photographic Memory.* Providence, RI: American Mathematical Society, 1987.

PÓLYA, GEORGE. *The Pólya Picture Album.* New York, NY: Birkhäuser, 1987.

3.7 Numbers and Algebra

* BECKMANN, PETR. *A History of π (pi),* Third Edition. Boulder, CO: Golem Press, 1970, 1974.

CRUMP, THOMAS. *The Anthropology of Numbers.* New York, NY: Cambridge University Press, 1990.

** DICKSON, LEONARD E. *History of the Theory of Numbers,* 3 Vols. New York, NY: Chelsea, 1952, 1971.

* MENNINGER, KARL. *Number Words and Number Symbols: A Cultural History of Numbers.* Cambridge, MA: MIT Press, 1977.

** VAN DER WAERDEN, B.L. *A History of Algebra: From al-Khwārizmī to Emmy Noether.* New York, NY: Springer-Verlag, 1985.

3.8 Calculus and Analysis

ARNOLD, V.I. *Huygens and Barrow, Newton and Hooke.* New York, NY: Birkhäuser, 1990.

* BARON, MARGARET E. *The Origins of the Infinitesimal Calculus.* Mineola, NY: Dover, 1987.

BOTTAZZINI, UMBERTO. *The Higher Calculus: A History of Real and Complex Analysis from Euler to Weierstrass.* New York, NY: Springer-Verlag, 1986.

** BOYER, CARL B. *The History of Calculus and Its Conceptual Development.* Mineola, NY: Dover, 1959.

*** EDWARDS, C.H., JR. *The Historical Development of the Calculus.* New York, NY: Springer-Verlag, 1979.

GRABINER, JUDITH V. *The Origins of Cauchy's Rigorous Calculus.* Cambridge, MA: MIT Press, 1981.

HALL, A. RUPERT. *Philosophers at War: The Quarrel Between Newton and Leibniz.* New York, NY: Cambridge University Press, 1980.

3.9 Geometry

BONOLA, ROBERTO. *Non-Euclidean Geometry: A Critical and Historical Study of Its Development.* Mineola, NY: Dover, 1955.

* BOYER, CARL B. *History of Analytic Geometry.* New York, NY: Scripta Mathematica, 1956; Princeton Junction, NJ: Scholar's Bookshelf, 1988.

* COOLIDGE, JULIAN L. *A History of the Conic Sections and Quadric Surfaces.* Oxford: Oxford University Press, 1945; Mineola, NY: Dover, 1968.

ROSENFELD, B.A. *A History of Non-Euclidean Geometry: Evolution of the Concept of a Geometric Space.* New York, NY: Springer-Verlag, 1988.

3.10 Probability and Statistics

ADAMS, WILLIAM J. *The Life and Times of the Central Limit Theorem.* New York, NY: Kaedmon, 1974.

COWLES, MICHAEL. *Statistics in Psychology: An Historical Perspective.* Hillsdale, NJ: Lawrence Erlbaum, 1989.

GANI, J., ED. *The Making of Statisticians.* New York, NY: Springer-Verlag, 1982.

** GIGERENZER, GERD, et al. *The Empire of Chance: How Probability Changed Science and Everyday Life.* New York, NY: Cambridge University Press, 1989.

HACKING, IAN. *The Emergence of Probability.* New York, NY: Cambridge University Press, 1975.

HALD, ANDERS. *A History of Probability and Statistics and Their Applications Before 1750.* New York, NY: John Wiley, 1990.

MAISTROV, LEONID E. *Probability Theory: A Historical Sketch.* New York, NY: Academic Press, 1974.

*** STIGLER, STEPHEN M. *The History of Statistics: The Measurement of Uncertainty Before 1900.* Cambridge, MA: Harvard University Press, 1986.

3.11 Computers

FREIBERGER, PAUL AND SWAINE, MICHAEL. *Fire in the Valley: The Making of the Personal Computer.* Berkeley, CA: Osborne/McGraw-Hill, 1984.

* GOLDSTINE, HERMAN H. *The Computer from Pascal to von Neumann.* Princeton, NJ: Princeton University Press, 1972, 1980.

LINDGREN, MICHAEL. *Glory and Failure.* Cambridge, MA: MIT Press, 1990.

4 Recreational Mathematics

4.1 Surveys

* AVERBACH, BONNIE AND CHEIN, ORIN. *Mathematics: Problem Solving through Recreational Mathematics.* New York, NY: W.H. Freeman, 1980.

*** BALL, W.W. ROUSE AND COXETER, H.S.M. *Mathematical Recreations and Essays*, Thirteenth Edition. Toronto: University of Toronto Press, 1974; Mineola, NY: Dover, 1987.

* BEILER, ALBERT. *Recreations in the Theory of Numbers.* Mineola, NY: Dover, 1964.

BERLEKAMP, ELWYN R.; CONWAY, JOHN HORTON; AND GUY, RICHARD K. *Winning Ways for Your Mathematical Plays*, 2 Vols. New York, NY: Academic Press, 1982.

*** KRAITCHIK, MAURICE. *Mathematical Recreations*, Second Edition. Mineola, NY: Dover, 1953.

** OGILVY, C. STANLEY. *Tomorrow's Math: Unsolved Problems for the Amateur*, Second Edition. New York, NY: Oxford University Press, 1972.

4.2 Games and Puzzles

* ANDREWS, WILLIAM S. *Magic Squares and Cubes,* Second Edition. Mineola, NY: Dover, 1960.

BRANDRETH, GYLES. *Numberplay.* New York, NY: Rawson, 1984.

* CARROLL, LEWIS. *Mathematical Recreations of Lewis Carroll,* 2 Vols. Mineola, NY: Dover, 1958.

DOMORYAD, A.P. *Mathematical Games and Pastimes.* Elmsford, NY: Pergamon Press, 1963.

* HORDERN, EDWARD. *Sliding Piece Puzzles.* New York, NY: Oxford University Press, 1986.

LINES, MALCOLM. *Think of a Number.* New York, NY: Adam Hilger, 1990.

STEWART, IAN. *Game, Set, and Math: Enigmas and Conundrums.* Cambridge, MA: Basil Blackwell, 1989.

4.3 Puzzle Collections

BARR, STEPHEN. *Mathematical Brain Benders: 2nd Miscellany of Puzzles.* Mineola, NY: Dover, 1982.

DUDENEY, HENRY E. *536 Puzzles and Curious Problems.* New York, NY: Charles Scribner's, 1967.

DUDENEY, HENRY E. *Amusements in Mathematics.* Mineola, NY: Dover, 1958.

*** GARDNER, MARTIN, ED. *The Mathematical Puzzles of Sam Loyd,* 2 Vols. Mineola, NY: Dover, 1959.

KORDEMSKY, BORIS A. *The Moscow Puzzles: 359 Mathematical Recreations.* New York, NY: Charles Scribner's, 1972.

* LOYD, SAM. *Sam Loyd's Cyclopedia of 5000 Puzzles, Tricks, and Conundrums.* New York, NY: Pinnacle, 1976.

NORTHROP, EUGENE P. *Riddles in Mathematics: A Book of Paradoxes.* Melbourne, FL: Robert E. Krieger, 1975.

* PHILLIPS, HUBERT. *My Best Puzzles in Logic and Reasoning.* Mineola, NY: Dover, 1961.

* PHILLIPS, HUBERT. *My Best Puzzles in Mathematics.* Mineola, NY: Dover, 1961.

SILVERMAN, DAVID L. *Your Move.* New York, NY: McGraw-Hill, 1971.

SMULLYAN, RAYMOND M. *The Lady or the Tiger? And Other Logic Puzzles.* New York, NY: Alfred A. Knopf, 1982.

4.4 Contests and Problems

ALEXANDERSON, GERALD L.; KLOSINSKI, LEONARD F.; AND LARSON, LOREN C., EDS. *The William Lowell Putnam Mathematical Competition: Problems and Solutions, 1965–1984.* Washington, DC: Mathematical Association of America, 1985.

** BARBEAU, EDWARD J.; KLAMKIN, MURRAY S.; AND MOSER, WILLIAM, EDS. *1001 Problems in High School Mathematics.* Montreal: Canadian Mathematical Congress, 1977.

* GLEASON, ANDREW M.; GREENWOOD, R.E.; AND KELLY, L.M. *The William Lowell Putnam Mathematical Competition: Problems and Solutions, 1938–1964.* Washington, DC: Mathematical Association of America, 1980.

GRAHAM, L.A. *Ingenious Mathematical Problems and Methods.* Mineola, NY: Dover, 1959.

GREITZER, SAMUEL L. *International Mathematical Olympiads, 1959–1977.* Washington, DC: Mathematical Association of America, 1978.

KLAMKIN, MURRAY S. *International Mathematical Olympiads, 1978–1985 and Forty Supplementary Problems.* Washington, DC: Mathematical Association of America, 1986.

** LARSON, LOREN C. *Problem-Solving Through Problems.* New York, NY: Springer-Verlag, 1983.

MBILI, L.S.R. *Mathematical Challenge! One Hundred Problems for the Olympiad Enthusiast.* Rondebosch, South Africa: Math Digest, 1978.

RUDERMAN, HARRY D., ED. *NYSML-ARML Contests, 1973–1985,* Second Edition. Reston, VA: National Council of Teachers of Mathematics, 1987.

** SALKIND, CHARLES T., et al., EDS. *Contest Problem Book,* 4 Vols. Washington, DC: Mathematical Association of America, 1961–83.

YAGLOM, A.M. AND YAGLOM, I.M. *Challenging Mathematical Programs with Elementary Solutions,* 2 Vols. Mineola, NY: Dover, 1987.

4.5 Martin Gardner

GARDNER, MARTIN. *Aha! Gotcha.* New York, NY: W.H. Freeman, 1982.

GARDNER, MARTIN. *Aha! Insight.* New York, NY: W.H. Freeman, 1978.

* GARDNER, MARTIN. *Hexaflexagons and Other Mathematical Diversions.* Chicago, IL: University of Chicago Press, 1988.

* GARDNER, MARTIN. *Knotted Doughnuts and Other Mathematical Entertainments.* New York, NY: W.H. Freeman, 1986.

* GARDNER, MARTIN. *Martin Gardner's New Mathematical Diversions from Scientific American.* Chicago, IL: University of Chicago Press, 1983.

GARDNER, MARTIN. *Mathematical Carnival.* Washington, DC: Mathematical Association of America, 1989.

* GARDNER, MARTIN. *Mathematical Magic Show.* New York, NY: Alfred A. Knopf, 1977; Washington, DC: Mathematical Association of America, 1990.

* GARDNER, MARTIN. *Penrose Tiles to Trapdoor Ciphers.* New York, NY: W.H. Freeman, 1989.

* GARDNER, MARTIN. *Riddles of the Sphinx And Other Mathematical Puzzle Tales.* Washington, DC: Mathematical Association of America, 1987.

GARDNER, MARTIN. *Science Fiction Puzzle Tales.* New York, NY: Clarkson N. Potter, 1981.

* GARDNER, MARTIN. *The Magic Numbers of Dr. Matrix.* Buffalo, NY: Prometheus Books, 1985.

GARDNER, MARTIN. *Time Travel and Other Mathematical Bewilderments.* New York, NY: W.H. Freeman, 1987.

GARDNER, MARTIN. *Wheels, Life, and Other Mathematical Amusements.* New York, NY: W.H. Freeman, 1983.

4.6 Miscellany

GARDINER, A. *Mathematical Puzzling.* New York, NY: Oxford University Press, 1987.

** GOLOMB, SOLOMON W. *Polyominoes.* New York, NY: Charles Scribner's, 1965.

KLARNER, DAVID A., ED. *The Mathematical Gardner.* Boston, MA: Prindle, Weber and Schmidt, 1981.

** LINDGREN, HARRY. *Geometric Dissections.* New York, NY: Van Nostrand Reinhold, 1964.

5 Education

5.1 Policy

HOWSON, A. GEOFFREY AND KAHANE, J.-P., EDS. *The Popularization of Mathematics.* New York, NY: Cambridge University Press, 1990.

KILPATRICK, JEREMY. *Academic Preparation in Mathematics: Teaching for Transition From High School to College.* New York, NY: College Board, 1985.

* MADISON, BERNARD L. AND HART, THERESE A. *A Challenge of Numbers: People in the Mathematical Sciences.* Washington, DC: National Academy Press, 1990.

** MATHEMATICAL SCIENCES EDUCATION BOARD. *Reshaping School Mathematics: A Philosophy and Framework for Curriculum.* Washington, DC: National Academy Press, 1990.

*** NATIONAL RESEARCH COUNCIL. *Everybody Counts: A Report to the Nation on the Future of Mathematics Education.* Washington, DC: National Academy Press, 1989.

*** NATIONAL RESEARCH COUNCIL. *Moving Beyond Myths: Revitalizing Undergraduate Mathematics.* Washington, DC: National Academy Press, 1991.

NATIONAL RESEARCH COUNCIL. *Renewing U.S. Mathematics: A Plan for the 1990s.* Washington, DC: National Academy Press, 1990.

NATIONAL RESEARCH COUNCIL. *Renewing U.S. Mathematics: Critical Resource for the Future.* Washington, DC: National Research Council, 1984.

*** STEEN, LYNN ARTHUR, ED. *On the Shoulders of Giants: New Approaches to Numeracy.* Washington, DC: National Academy Press, 1990.

5.2 Philosophy

ERNEST, PAUL. *The Philosophy of Mathematics Education.* New York, NY: Falmer Press, 1991.

FREUDENTHAL, HANS. *Mathematics as an Educational Task.* Norwell, MA: D. Reidel, 1973.

MELLIN-OLSEN, STEIG. *The Politics of Mathematics Education: Mathematics Education Library.* Norwell, MA: D. Reidel, 1987.

5.3 Psychology

NESHER, PEARLA AND KILPATRICK, JEREMY, EDS. *Mathematics and Cognition.* New York, NY: Cambridge University Press, 1990.

PIAGET, JEAN.; INHELDER, B.; AND SZEMINSKA, A. *The Child's Conception of Geometry.* New York, NY: Harper Torchbooks, 1964.

* PIAGET, JEAN. *The Child's Conception of Number.* New York, NY: W.W. Norton, 1965.

* RESNICK, LAUREN B. AND FORD, WENDY W. *The Psychology of Mathematics for Instruction.* Hillsdale, NJ: Lawrence Erlbaum, 1981.

SCHOENFELD, ALAN H., ED. *Cognitive Science and Mathematics Education.* Hillsdale, NJ: Lawrence Erlbaum, 1987.

* SKEMP, RICHARD R. *The Psychology of Learning Mathematics,* Second Edition. New York, NY: Penguin, 1973; Hillsdale, NJ: Lawrence Erlbaum, 1986.

5.4 Culture

ASCHER, MARCIA AND ASCHER, ROBERT. *Code of the Quipu: A Study in Media, Mathematics, and Culture.* Ann Arbor, MI: University of Michigan Press, 1981.

* ASCHER, MARCIA. *Ethnomathematics: A Multicultural View of Mathematical Ideas.* Pacific Grove, CA: Brooks/Cole, 1991.

BISHOP, ALAN J. *Mathematical Enculturation: A Cultural Perspective on Mathematics Education.* Norwell, MA: Kluwer Academic, 1988.

CLOSS, MICHAEL P., ED. *Native American Mathematics.* Austin, TX: University of Texas Press, 1986.

COCKING, R.R. AND MESTRE, JOSE P., EDS. *Linguistic and Cultural Influences on Learning Mathematics.* Hillsdale, NJ: Lawrence Erlbaum, 1988.

* ZASLAVSKY, CLAUDIA. *Africa Counts: Number and Pattern in African Culture.* Boston, MA: Prindle, Weber and Schmidt, 1973.

5.5 History

* BAUMGART, JOHN K. *Historical Topics for the Mathematics Classroom.* Reston, VA: National Council of Teachers of Mathematics, 1969, 1989.

BIDWELL, JAMES K. AND CLASON, ROBERT G., EDS. *Readings in the History of Mathematics Education.* Reston, VA: National Council of Teachers of Mathematics, 1970.

COHEN, PATRICIA CLINE. *A Calculating People: The Spread of Numeracy in Early America.* Chicago, IL: University of Chicago Press, 1982.

JONES, PHILLIP S., ED. *A History of Mathematics Education in the United States and Canada: 32nd Yearbook.* Reston, VA: National Council of Teachers of Mathematics, 1970.

5.6 Curriculum and Instruction

* AMERICAN ASSOCIATION FOR THE ADVANCEMENT OF SCIENCE. *Science For All Americans.* Washington, DC: American Association for the Advancement of Science, 1989.

ATHEN, HERMANN AND HEINZ, KUNLE, EDS. *Proceedings of the Third International Congress on Mathematical Education.* Karlsruhe, Germany: Zentralblatt für Didaktik der Mathematik, 1977.

* BLACKWELL, DAVID AND HENKIN, LEON. *Mathematics: Report of the Project 2061 Phase I Mathematics Panel.* Washington, DC: American Association for the Advancement of Science, 1989.

CARSS, MARJORIE, ED. *Proceedings of the Fifth International Congress on Mathematical Education.* New York, NY: Birkhäuser, 1986.

* COMMITTEE ON MATHEMATICAL EDUCATION OF TEACHERS. *Guidelines for the Continuing Mathematical Education of Teachers.* Washington, DC: Mathematical Association of America, 1988.

CONFERENCE BOARD OF THE MATHEMATICAL SCIENCES. *Overview and Analysis of School Mathematics, Grades K–12.* Washington, DC: Conference Board of the Mathematical Sciences, 1975.

** COONEY, THOMAS J., ED. *Teaching and Learning Mathematics in the 1990s: 1990 Yearbook.* Reston, VA: National Council of Teachers of Mathematics, 1990.

* DAVIDSON, NEIL, ED. *Cooperative Learning in Mathematics: A Handbook for Teachers.* Reading, MA: Addison-Wesley, 1990.

HIRST, ANN AND HIRST, KEITH, EDS. *Proceedings of the Sixth International Congress on Mathematical Education.* Budapest: János Bolyai Mathematical Society, 1988.

HOWSON, A. GEOFFREY, ED. *Developments in Mathematical Education: Proceedings of the Second International Congress on Mathematical Education.* New York, NY: Cambridge University Press, 1973.

HOWSON, A. GEOFFREY; KEITEL, CHRISTINE; AND KILPATRICK, JEREMY. *Curriculum Development in Mathematics.* New York, NY: Cambridge University Press, 1981.

* LINDQUIST, MARY M. AND SHULTE, ALBERT P. *Learning and Teaching Geometry, K–12: 1987 Yearbook.* Reston, VA: National Council of Teachers of Mathematics, 1987.

** NATIONAL COUNCIL OF TEACHERS OF MATHEMATICS. *A Sourcebook of Applications of School Mathematics.* Reston, VA: National Council of Teachers of Mathematics, 1980.

*** NATIONAL COUNCIL OF TEACHERS OF MATHEMATICS. *Curriculum and Evaluation Standards for School Mathematics.* Reston, VA: National Council of Teachers of Mathematics, 1989.

*** NATIONAL COUNCIL OF TEACHERS OF MATHEMATICS. *Professional Standards for Teaching Mathematics.* Reston, VA: National Council of Teachers of Mathematics, 1991.

SCHOEN, HAROLD L. AND ZWENG, MARILYN J. *Estimation and Mental Computation: 1986 Yearbook.* Reston, VA: National Council of Teachers of Mathematics, 1986.

SHULTE, ALBERT P., ED. *Teaching Statistics and Probability: 1981 Yearbook.* Reston, VA: National Council of Teachers of Mathematics, 1981.

* SILVER, EDWARD A.; KILPATRICK, JEREMY; AND SCHLESINGER, B. *Thinking Through Mathematics: Fostering Inquiry and Communication in Mathematics Classrooms.* New York, NY: College Board, 1990.

STEEN, LYNN ARTHUR AND ALBERS, DONALD J., EDS. *Teaching Teachers, Teaching Students: Reflections on Mathematical Education.* New York, NY: Birkhäuser, 1981.

TAYLOR, ROSS, ED. *Professional Development for Teachers of Mathematics: A Handbook.* Reston, VA: National Council of Teachers of Mathematics, 1986.

TOBIAS, SHEILA. *Overcoming Math Anxiety.* New York, NY: W.W. Norton, 1978; Boston, MA: Houghton Mifflin, 1980.

TOBIAS, SHEILA. *Succeed With Math: Every Student's Guide to Conquering Math Anxiety.* New York, NY: College Board, 1987.

ZWENG, MARILYN J., et al., EDS. *Proceedings of the Fourth International Congress on Mathematical Education.* New York, NY: Birkhäuser, 1983.

5.7 Elementary Education

BAROODY, A.J. *A Guide to Teaching Mathematics in the Primary Grades.* Needham Heights, MA: Allyn and Bacon, 1989.

BURNS, MARILYN. *The I Hate Mathematics! Book.* Waltham, MA: Little, Brown, 1975.

PAYNE, JOSEPH N., ED. *Mathematics For the Young Child*. Reston, VA: National Council of Teachers of Mathematics, 1990.

POST, THOMAS R., ED. *Teaching Mathematics in Grades K-8: Research Based Methods*. Needham Heights, MA: Allyn and Bacon, 1988.

* TRAFTON, PAUL R. AND SHULTE, ALBERT P., EDS. *New Directions for Elementary School Mathematics: 1989 Yearbook*. Reston, VA: National Council of Teachers of Mathematics, 1989.

* WORTH, JOAN, ED. *Preparing Elementary School Mathematics Teachers: Readings from the Arithmetic Teacher*. Reston, VA: National Council of Teachers of Mathematics, 1987.

5.8 Secondary Education

** CAMPBELL, PAUL J. AND GRINSTEIN, LOUISE S. *Mathematics Education in Secondary Schools and Two-Year Colleges: A Sourcebook*. New York, NY: Garland, 1988.

* COXFORD, ARTHUR F. AND SHULTE, ALBERT P. *The Ideas of Algebra, K-12: 1988 Yearbook*. Reston, VA: National Council of Teachers of Mathematics, 1988.

DALTON, LEROY C. AND SNYDER, HENRY D., EDS. *Topics for Mathematics Clubs*. Reston, VA: National Council of Teachers of Mathematics, 1983.

EASTERDAY, KENNETH E.; HENRY, LOREN L.; AND SIMPSON, F. MORGAN. *Activities for Junior High School and Middle School Mathematics*. Reston, VA: National Council of Teachers of Mathematics, 1981.

HIRSCH, CHRISTIAN R. AND ZWENG, MARILYN J. *The Secondary School Mathematics Curriculum: 1985 Yearbook*. Reston, VA: National Council of Teachers of Mathematics, 1985.

* SOBEL, MAX A., ED. *Readings for Enrichment in Secondary School Mathematics*. Reston, VA: National Council of Teachers of Mathematics, 1988.

5.9 Undergraduate Education

** ALBERS, DONALD J., et al. *A Statistical Abstract of Undergraduate Programs in the Mathematical and Computer Sciences, 1990-91*. Washington, DC: Mathematical Association of America, 1992.

*** ALBERS, DONALD J.; RODI, STEPHEN B.; AND WATKINS, ANN E., EDS. *New Directions in Two-Year College Mathematics*. New York, NY: Springer-Verlag, 1985.

** COMMITTEE ON THE UNDERGRADUATE PROGRAM IN MATHEMATICS. *Reshaping College Mathematics*. Washington, DC: Mathematical Association of America, 1989.

* DAVIS, RONALD M., ED. *A Curriculum in Flux: Mathematics at Two-Year Colleges*. Washington, DC: Mathematical Association of America, 1989.

*** DOUGLAS, RONALD G., ED. *Toward A Lean and Lively Calculus*. Washington, DC: Mathematical Association of America, 1986.

KNUTH, DONALD E.; LARRABEE, TRACY; AND ROBERTS, PAUL M. *Mathematical Writing*. Washington, DC: Mathematical Association of America, 1989.

* LEINBACH, L. CARL, et al. *The Laboratory Approach to Teaching Calculus*. Washington, DC: Mathematical Association of America, 1991.

*** LEITZEL, JAMES R.C., ED. *A Call For Change: Recommendations for the Mathematical Preparation of Teachers of Mathematics*. Washington, DC: Mathematical Association of America, 1991.

RALSTON, ANTHONY AND YOUNG, GAIL S., EDS. *The Future of College Mathematics*. New York, NY: Springer-Verlag, 1983.

RALSTON, ANTHONY, ED. *Discrete Mathematics in the First Two Years*. Washington, DC: Mathematical Association of America, 1989.

** SCHOENFELD, ALAN H., ED. *A Sourcebook for College Mathematics Teaching*. Washington, DC: Mathematical Association of America, 1990.

* SENECHAL, LESTER, ED. *Models for Undergraduate Research in Mathematics*. Washington, DC: Mathematical Association of America, 1990.

** SMITH, DAVID A., et al., EDS. *Computers and Mathematics: The Use of Computers in Undergraduate Instruction*. Washington, DC: Mathematical Association of America, 1988.

*** STEEN, LYNN ARTHUR, ED. *Calculus for a New Century: A Pump, Not a Filter.* Washington, DC: Mathematical Association of America, 1988.

** STERRETT, ANDREW, ED. *Using Writing to Teach Mathematics.* Washington, DC: Mathematical Association of America, 1990.

* TOBIAS, SHEILA. *They're Not Dumb, They're Different: Stalking the Second Tier.* Tucson, AZ: Research Corporation, 1990.

*** TUCKER, THOMAS W., ED. *Priming the Calculus Pump: Innovations and Resources.* Washington, DC: Mathematical Association of America, 1990.

** ZIMMERMANN, WALTER AND CUNNINGHAM, STEVE, EDS. *Visualization in Teaching and Learning Mathematics.* Washington, DC: Mathematical Association of America, 1991.

5.10 Minorities and Women

CROWLEY, MICHAEL F. AND LANE, MELISSA J., EDS. *Women and Minorities in Science and Engineering.* Washington, DC: National Science Foundation, 1986.

** FENNEMA, ELIZABETH AND LEDER, GILAH, EDS. *Mathematics and Gender.* New York, NY: Teachers College Press, 1990.

* GRINSTEIN, LOUISE S. AND CAMPBELL, PAUL J., EDS. *Women of Mathematics: A Biobibliographic Sourcebook.* Westport, CT: Greenwood Press, 1987.

* KENSCHAFT, PATRICIA C. AND KEITH, SANDRA, EDS. *Winning Women Into Mathematics.* Washington, DC: Mathematical Association of America, 1991.

* NEWELL, VIRGINIA K., *et al.*, EDS. *Black Mathematicians and Their Works.* Ardmore, PA: Dorrance, 1980.

* ORR, ELEANOR WILSON. *Twice As Less: Black English and the Performance of Black Students in Mathematics and Science.* New York, NY: W.W. Norton, 1987.

* OSEN, L.M. *Women in Mathematics.* Cambridge, MA: MIT Press, 1974.

PERL, T.H. *Math Equals.* Reading, MA: Addison-Wesley, 1978.

SAMMONS, VIVIAN O. *Blacks in Science and Medicine.* New York, NY: Hemisphere, 1990.

5.11 Problem Solving

BROWN, STEPHEN I. AND WALTER, MARION I. *The Art of Problem Posing.* Philadelphia, PA: Franklin Institute Press, 1983.

CHARLES, RANDALL I.; LESTER, FRANK; AND O'DAFFER, PHARES G. *How To Evaluate Progress in Problem Solving.* Reston, VA: National Council of Teachers of Mathematics, 1987.

MASON, JOHN H.; BURTON, LEONE; AND STACEY, KAYE. *Thinking Mathematically.* Reading, MA: Addison-Wesley, 1982, 1985.

MASON, JOHN H. *Learning and Doing Mathematics.* Houndmills, England: Macmillan Education, 1988.

MCLEOD, DOUGLAS AND ADAMS, V., EDS. *Affect and Mathematical Problem Solving: A New Perspective.* New York, NY: Springer-Verlag, 1989.

*** PÓLYA, GEORGE. *How To Solve It*, Second Edition. Princeton, NJ: Princeton University Press, 1945; New York, NY: Doubleday, 1957.

** PÓLYA, GEORGE. *Mathematical Discovery: On Understanding, Learning, and Teaching Problem Solving*, Combined Edition. New York, NY: John Wiley, 1962, 1981.

* PÓLYA, GEORGE. *Mathematics and Plausible Reasoning*, 2 Vols. Princeton, NJ: Princeton University Press, 1954, 1969.

RUBINSTEIN, MOSHE F. *Patterns of Problem Solving.* Englewood Cliffs, NJ: Prentice Hall, 1975.

** SCHOENFELD, ALAN H. *Mathematical Problem Solving.* New York, NY: Academic Press, 1985.

* SCHOENFELD, ALAN H. *Problem Solving in the Mathematics Curriculum: A Report, Recommendations, and an Annotated Bibliography.* Washington, DC: Mathematical Association of America, 1983.

5.12 Research and Research Summaries

* CHARLES, RANDALL I. AND SILVER, EDWARD A., EDS. *The Teaching and Assessing of Mathematical Problem Solving.* Hillsdale, NJ: Lawrence Erlbaum, 1988; Reston, VA: National Council of Teachers of Mathematics, 1988.

* GROUWS, DOUGLAS A.; COONEY, THOMAS J.; AND JONES, DOUGLAS, EDS. *Perspectives on Research on Effective Mathematics Teaching.* Hillsdale, NJ: Lawrence Erlbaum, 1988; Reston, VA: National Council of Teachers of Mathematics, 1988.

HIEBERT, JAMES AND BEHR, MERLYN, EDS. *Number Concepts and Operations in the Middle Grades.* Hillsdale, NJ: Lawrence Erlbaum, 1988; Reston, VA: National Council of Teachers of Mathematics, 1988.

RESNICK, LAUREN B. AND KLOPFER, L.E., EDS. *Toward the Thinking Curriculum: Current Cognitive Research.* Alexandria, VA: Association for Supervision and Curriculum Development, 1989.

*** RESNICK, LAUREN B. *Education and Learning to Think.* Washington, DC: National Academy Press, 1987.

* WAGNER, SIGRID AND KIERAN, CAROLYN, EDS. *Research Issues in the Learning and Teaching of Algebra.* Hillsdale, NJ: Lawrence Erlbaum, 1989; Reston, VA: National Council of Teachers of Mathematics, 1989.

5.13 Studies and Assessment

** DOSSEY, JOHN A., et al. *The Mathematics Report Card: Are We Measuring Up?* Princeton, NJ: Educational Testing Service, 1988.

KULM, GERALD, ED. *Assessing Higher Order Thinking in Mathematics.* Washington, DC: American Association for the Advancement of Science, 1990.

LAPOINTE, ARCHIE; MEAD, NANCY; AND PHILLIPS, GARY. *A World of Differences: An International Assessment of Mathematics and Science.* Princeton, NJ: Educational Testing Service, 1989.

LINDQUIST, MARY M., ED. *Results from the Fourth Mathematics Assessment of the National Assessment of Educational Progress.* Reston, VA: National Council of Teachers of Mathematics, 1989.

MCKNIGHT, CURTIS C., et al. *The Underachieving Curriculum: Assessing U.S. School Mathematics From An International Perspective.* Champaign, IL: Stipes, 1987.

* ROMBERG, THOMAS A., ED. *Mathematics Assessment and Evaluation: Imperatives for Mathematics Educators.* Albany, NY: SUNY Press, 1991.

STEVENSON, HAROLD W., et al. *Making the Grade in Mathematics: Elementary School Mathematics in the United States, Taiwan, and Japan.* Reston, VA: National Council of Teachers of Mathematics, 1990.

STIGLER, JAMES W.; LEE, SHIN-YING; AND STEVENSON, HAROLD W. *Mathematical Knowledge of Japanese, Chinese, and American Elementary School Children.* Reston, VA: National Council of Teachers of Mathematics, 1990.

5.14 Computers and Technology

* CHAZAN, DANIEL AND HOUDE, RICHARD. *How to Use Conjecturing and Microcomputers to Teach Geometry.* Reston, VA: National Council of Teachers of Mathematics, 1989.

FEY, JAMES T., ED. *Computing and Mathematics: The Impact on Secondary School Curricula.* Reston, VA: National Council of Teachers of Mathematics, 1984.

HANSEN, VIGGO P. AND ZWENG, MARILYN J. *Computers in Mathematics Education: 1984 Yearbook.* Reston, VA: National Council of Teachers of Mathematics, 1984.

HOWSON, A. GEOFFREY AND KAHANE, J.-P., EDS. *The Influence of Computers and Informatics on Mathematics and Its Teaching.* New York, NY: Cambridge University Press, 1986.

* PAPERT, SEYMOUR. *Mindstorms: Children, Computers, and Powerful Ideas.* New York, NY: Basic Books, 1980.

6 Calculus and Precalculus

6.1 School Mathematics

ALLENDOERFER, C.B. AND OAKLEY, C.O. *Principles of Mathematics.* New York, NY: McGraw-Hill, 1963.

AUSLANDER, LOUIS. *What Are Numbers?* Glenview, IL: Scott Foresman, 1969.

* MARTIN, EDWARD, ED. *Elements of Mathematics, Book B: Problem Book.* St. Louis, MO: CEMREL-CSMP, 1975.

SEYMOUR, DALE. *Visual Patterns in Pascal's Triangle.* Palo Alto, CA: Dale Seymour, 1986.

6.2 Precalculus

COHEN, DAVID. *Precalculus,* Third Edition. St. Paul, MN: West, 1984, 1989.

COXFORD, ARTHUR F. AND PAYNE, JOSEPH N. *Advanced Mathematics: A Preparation for Calculus.* San Diego, CA: Harcourt Brace Jovanovich, 1984.

DEMANA, FRANKLIN D. AND LEITZEL, JOAN R. *Transition to College Mathematics.* Reading, MA: Addison-Wesley, 1984.

** DEMANA, FRANKLIN D. AND WAITS, BERT K. *Precalculus Mathematics—A Graphing Approach.* Reading, MA: Addison-Wesley, 1990.

*** DEMANA, FRANKLIN D., et al. *Graphing Calculator and Computer Graphing Laboratory Manual,* Second Edition. Reading, MA: Addison-Wesley, 1991.

FOERSTER, PAUL A. *Precalculus with Trigonometry: Functions and Applications.* Reading, MA: Addison-Wesley, 1987.

GROSSMAN, STANLEY I. *Algebra and Trigonometry.* Philadelphia, PA: Saunders College, 1989.

KAUFMANN, JEROME E. *College Algebra and Trigonometry,* Second Edition. Boston, MA: PWS-Kent, 1987, 1990.

LARSON, LOREN C. *Algebra and Trigonometry Refresher for Calculus Students.* New York, NY: W.H. Freeman, 1979.

* LEITHOLD, LOUIS. *Before Calculus: Functions, Graphs, and Analytic Geometry,* Second Edition. New York, NY: Harper and Row, 1985, 1989.

* LEWIS, PHILIP G. *Approaching Precalculus Mathematics Discretely: Explorations in a Computer Environment.* Cambridge, MA: MIT Press, 1990.

*** NORTH CAROLINA SCHOOL OF SCIENCE AND TECHNOLOGY. *Contemporary Precalculus Through Applications.* Providence, RI: Janson, 1991.

SIMMONS, GEORGE F. *Precalculus Mathematics in a Nutshell: Geometry, Algebra, Trigonometry.* Los Altos, CA: William Kaufmann, 1981.

SOBEL, MAX A. AND LERNER, NORBERT. *Algebra and Trigonometry: A Pre-Calculus Approach,* Third Edition. Englewood Cliffs, NJ: Prentice Hall, 1983, 1991.

SWOKOWSKI, EARL W. *Algebra and Trigonometry with Analytic Geometry,* Seventh Edition. Boston, MA: PWS-Kent, 1989.

USISKIN, ZALMAN. *Advanced Algebra with Transformations and Applications.* River Forest, IL: Laidlaw Brothers, 1976.

6.3 Elementary Calculus

** ANTON, HOWARD. *Calculus with Analytic Geometry,* Third Edition. New York, NY: John Wiley, 1980, 1988.

ASH, CAROL AND ASH, ROBERT B. *The Calculus Tutoring Book.* Los Angeles, CA: IEEE Computer Society, 1985.

BITTINGER, MARVIN L. *Calculus: A Modeling Approach,* Fourth Edition. Reading, MA: Addison-Wesley, 1980, 1988.

FINNEY, ROSS L. AND THOMAS, GEORGE B., JR. *Calculus.* Reading, MA: Addison-Wesley, 1990.

* Goldstein, Larry J.; Lay, David C.; and Schneider, David I. *Calculus and Its Applications,* Fifth Edition. Englewood Cliffs, NJ: Prentice Hall, 1977, 1990.

Grossman, Stanley I. *Calculus,* Fourth Edition. New York, NY: Academic Press, 1981; San Diego, CA: Harcourt Brace Jovanovich, 1988.

Hamming, Richard W. *Methods of Mathematics Applied to Calculus, Probability, and Statistics.* Englewood Cliffs, NJ: Prentice Hall, 1985.

Keisler, H. Jerome. *Elementary Calculus,* Second Edition. Boston, MA: Prindle, Weber and Schmidt, 1976, 1986.

* Kline, Morris. *Calculus: An Intuitive and Physical Approach,* Second Edition. New York, NY: John Wiley, 1977.

Levi, Howard. *Polynomials, Power Series, and Calculus.* New York, NY: Van Nostrand Reinhold, 1968.

** Marsden, Jerrold E. and Weinstein, Alan. *Calculus,* Second Edition. Redwood City, CA: Benjamin Cummings, 1980; New York, NY: Springer-Verlag, 1985.

** Priestley, William M. *Calculus: An Historical Approach.* New York, NY: Springer-Verlag, 1979.

Simmons, George F. *Calculus with Analytic Geometry.* New York, NY: McGraw-Hill, 1985.

Small, Donald B. and Hosack, John M. *Calculus: An Integrated Approach.* New York, NY: McGraw-Hill, 1990.

Small, Donald B. and Hosack, John M. *Explorations in Calculus with a Computer Algebra System.* New York, NY: McGraw-Hill, 1990.

** Stein, Sherman K. *Calculus and Analytic Geometry,* Fourth Edition. New York, NY: McGraw-Hill, 1982, 1987.

** Strang, Gilbert. *Calculus.* Wellesley, MA: Wellesley-Cambridge Press, 1991.

Swokowski, Earl W. *Calculus,* Fifth Edition. Boston, MA: PWS-Kent, 1975, 1991.

*** Thomas, George B., Jr. and Finney, Ross L. *Calculus and Analytic Geometry,* Seventh Edition. Reading, MA: Addison-Wesley, 1968, 1987.

6.4 Advanced Calculus

* Apostol, Tom M. *Calculus,* 2 Vols., Second Edition. New York, NY: John Wiley, 1967, 1969.

* Bressoud, David M. *Second Year Calculus.* New York, NY: Springer-Verlag, 1991.

Buck, R. Creighton. *Advanced Calculus,* Third Edition. New York, NY: McGraw-Hill, 1965, 1978.

Courant, Richard and John, Fritz. *Introduction to Calculus and Analysis,* 2 Vols. New York, NY: John Wiley, 1965; New York, NY: Springer-Verlag, 1989.

Courant, Richard. *Differential and Integral Calculus,* 2 Vols. New York, NY: Interscience, 1937.

Knopp, Konrad. *Infinite Sequences and Series.* Mineola, NY: Dover, 1956.

Knopp, Konrad. *Theory and Application of Infinite Series.* New York, NY: Hafner Press, 1948; Mineola, NY: Dover, 1990.

** Marsden, Jerrold E. and Weinstein, Alan. *Calculus III,* Second Edition. New York, NY: Springer-Verlag, 1985.

** Schey, H.M. *Div, Grad, Curl, and All That: An Informal Text on Vector Calculus.* New York, NY: W.W. Norton, 1973.

Williamson, Richard E.; Crowell, Richard H.; and Trotter, Hale F. *Calculus of Vector Functions,* Third Edition. Englewood Cliffs, NJ: Prentice Hall, 1972.

6.5 Supplementary Resources

Apostol, Tom M., *et al.*, eds. *Selected Papers on Calculus.* Washington, DC: Mathematical Association of America, 1969.

Apostol, Tom M., *et al.*, eds. *Selected Papers on Precalculus.* Washington, DC: Mathematical Association of America, 1977.

** Cipra, Barry. *Misteaks ... and How to Find Them Before the Teacher Does ...,* Second Edition. New York, NY: Birkhäuser, 1983; New York, NY: Academic Press, 1989.

  * DE MESTRE, NEVILLE. *The Mathematics of Projectiles in Sport.* New York, NY: Cambridge University Press, 1990.

  * GRINSTEIN, LOUISE S. AND MICHAELS, BRENDA, EDS. *Calculus: Readings from the Mathematics Teacher.* Reston, VA: National Council of Teachers of Mathematics, 1977.

   MAY, KENNETH O., ED. *Lectures on Calculus.* San Francisco, CA: Holden-Day, 1967.

   MENDELSON, ELLIOTT. *Schaum's 3000 Solved Problems in Calculus.* New York, NY: McGraw-Hill, 1988.

   OGILVY, C. STANLEY. *A Calculus Notebook.* Boston, MA: Prindle, Weber and Schmidt, 1968.

*** SAWYER, W.W. *What is Calculus About?* Washington, DC: Mathematical Association of America, 1975.

   SWANN, HOWARD AND JOHNSON, JOHN. *Prof. E. McSquared's Expanded Intergalactic Version: A Calculus Primer.* Providence, RI: Janson, 1989.

  * TOEPLITZ, OTTO. *Calculus: A Genetic Approach.* Chicago, IL: University of Chicago Press, 1963.

7 Differential Equations

7.1 Introductory Texts

*** BOYCE, WILLIAM E. AND DIPRIMA, RICHARD C. *Elementary Differential Equations and Boundary Value Problems,* Fifth Edition. New York, NY: John Wiley, 1969, 1992.

   BRAUN, MARTIN. *Differential Equations and Their Applications: An Introduction to Applied Mathematics,* Third Edition. New York, NY: Springer-Verlag, 1975, 1983.

  * EDWARDS, C.H., JR. AND PENNEY, DAVID E. *Elementary Differential Equations with Applications,* Second Edition. Englewood Cliffs, NJ: Prentice Hall, 1985, 1989.

   HUBBARD, JOHN H. AND WEST, BEVERLY H. *Differential Equations: A Dynamical Systems Approach,* New York, NY: Springer-Verlag, 1991.

   MILLER, RICHARD K. *Ordinary Differential Equations.* New York, NY: Academic Press, 1982.

 ** REDHEFFER, RAY AND PORT, DAN. *Differential Equations: Theory and Applications.* Boston, MA: Jones and Bartlett, 1991.

   SIMMONS, GEORGE F. AND ROBERTSON, JOHN S. *Differential Equations with Applications and Historical Notes,* Second Edition. New York, NY: McGraw-Hill, 1972, 1991.

  * ZILL, DENNIS G. *A First Course in Differential Equations with Applications,* Fourth Edition. Boston, MA: PWS-Kent, 1980, 1989.

7.2 Advanced Topics

  * ARROWSMITH, D.K. AND PLACE, C.M. *An Introduction to Dynamical Systems.* New York, NY: Cambridge University Press, 1990.

   BIRKHOFF, GARRETT AND ROTA, GIAN-CARLO. *Ordinary Differential Equations,* Fourth Edition. New York, NY: John Wiley, 1969, 1989.

  * CHURCHILL, RUEL V. AND BROWN, JAMES W. *Fourier Series and Boundary Value Problems,* Third Edition. New York, NY: McGraw-Hill, 1978.

 ** CODDINGTON, EARL A. AND LEVINSON, NORMAN. *Theory of Ordinary Differential Equations.* New York, NY: McGraw-Hill, 1955; Melbourne, FL: Robert E. Krieger, 1984.

  * HIRSCH, MORRIS W. AND SMALE, STEPHEN. *Differential Equations, Dynamical Systems, and Linear Algebra.* New York, NY: Academic Press, 1974.

  * IOOSS, GÉRARD AND JOSEPH, DANIEL D. *Elementary Stability and Bifurcation Theory,* Second Edition. New York, NY: Springer-Verlag, 1990.

   JOHN, FRITZ. *Partial Differential Equations,* Fourth Edition. New York, NY: Springer-Verlag, 1971, 1982.

** Wiggins, Stephen. *Introduction to Applied Nonlinear Dynamical Systems and Chaos.* New York, NY: Springer-Verlag, 1990.

8 Analysis

8.1 Foundations of Analysis

Landau, Edmund G.H. *The Foundations of Analysis*, Third Edition. New York, NY: Chelsea, 1951, 1966.

Smith, D.; Eggen, M.; and St. Andre, R. *A Transition to Advanced Mathematics*, Third Edition. Pacific Grove, CA: Brooks/Cole, 1990.

** Solow, Daniel. *How To Read and Do Proofs: An Introduction to Mathematical Thought Processes*, Second Edition. New York, NY: John Wiley, 1982, 1990.

8.2 Real Analysis

Apostol, Tom M. *Mathematical Analysis*, Second Edition. Reading, MA: Addison-Wesley, 1974.

Bartle, Robert G. *Elements of Real Analysis*, Second Edition. New York, NY: John Wiley, 1976.

*** Gelbaum, Bernard R. and Olmsted, John M.H. *Theorems and Counterexamples in Mathematics.* (Former title: *Counterexamples in Analysis.*) San Francisco, CA: Holden-Day, 1964; New York, NY: Springer-Verlag, 1990.

Hewitt, Edwin and Stromberg, Karl R. *Real and Abstract Analysis: A Modern Treatment of the Theory of Functions of a Real Variable.* New York, NY: Springer-Verlag, 1969, 1975.

Kolmogorov, Andrei N. and Fomin, S.V. *Introductory Real Analysis.* Mineola, NY: Dover, 1975.

Protter, Murray H. and Morrey, C.B. *A First Course in Real Analysis.* New York, NY: Springer-Verlag, 1977.

* Ross, Kenneth A. *Elementary Analysis: The Theory of Calculus.* New York, NY: Springer-Verlag, 1980.

Royden, H.L. *Real Analysis*, Third Edition. New York, NY: Macmillan, 1968, 1988.

** Rudin, Walter. *Principles of Mathematical Analysis*, Third Edition. New York, NY: McGraw-Hill, 1953, 1976.

8.3 Fractals

*** Barnsley, Michael. *Fractals Everywhere.* New York, NY: Academic Press, 1988.

* Devaney, Robert L. and Keen, Linda, eds. *Chaos and Fractals: The Mathematics Behind the Computer Graphics.* Providence, RI: American Mathematical Society, 1989.

Devaney, Robert L. *An Introduction to Chaotic Dynamical Systems*, Second Edition. Redwood City, CA: Benjamin Cummings, 1986, 1989.

*** Devaney, Robert L. *Chaos, Fractals, and Dynamics: Computer Experiments in Mathematics.* Reading, MA: Addison-Wesley, 1990.

* Lauwerier, Hans. *Fractals: Endlessly Repeated Geometrical Figures.* Princeton, NJ: Princeton University Press, 1991.

* Mandelbrot, Benoit. *The Fractal Geometry of Nature.* New York, NY: W.H. Freeman, 1982.

** Peitgen, Heinz-Otto and Richter, P.H. *The Beauty of Fractals: Images of Complex Dynamical Systems.* New York, NY: Springer-Verlag, 1986.

Peitgen, Heinz-Otto and Saupe, Dietmar, eds. *The Science of Fractal Images.* New York, NY: Springer-Verlag, 1988.

Schroeder, Manfred R. *Fractals, Chaos, Power Laws: Minutes from an Infinite Paradise.* New York, NY: W.H. Freeman, 1990.

8.4 Complex Analysis

AHLFORS, LARS V. *Complex Analysis: An Introduction to the Theory of Analytic Functions of One Complex Variable,* Third Edition. New York, NY: McGraw-Hill, 1966, 1979.

KNOPP, KONRAD. *Theory of Functions,* 2 Vols. Mineola, NY: Dover, 1945, 1947; 1968.

* KRANTZ, STEVEN G. *Complex Analysis: The Geometric Viewpoint.* Washington, DC: Mathematical Association of America, 1990.

PÓLYA, GEORGE AND LATTA, GORDON. *Complex Variables.* New York, NY: John Wiley, 1974.

** REMMERT, REINHOLD. *Theory of Complex Functions.* New York, NY: Springer-Verlag, 1991.

RUDIN, WALTER. *Real and Complex Analysis,* Third Edition. New York, NY: McGraw-Hill, 1974, 1987.

8.5 Functional Analysis

* BANACH, STEFAN. *Theory of Linear Operators.* Warsaw: 1932; New York, NY: Elsevier Science, 1987.

GOFFMAN, CASPER AND PEDRICK, GEORGE. *A First Course in Functional Analysis,* Second Edition. Englewood Cliffs, NJ: Prentice Hall, 1965; New York, NY: Chelsea, 1983.

LIUSTERNIK, L. AND SOBOLEV, V. *Elements of Functional Analysis.* New York, NY: Frederick Ungar, 1961.

RIESZ, FRIGYES AND NAGY, BELA SZ. *Functional Analysis.* New York, NY: Frederick Ungar, 1955; Mineola, NY: Dover, 1990.

8.6 Special Topics

AKHIEZER, N.I. *Elements of the Theory of Elliptic Functions.* Providence, RI: American Mathematical Society, 1990.

* BECKENBACH, EDWIN F. AND BELLMAN, RICHARD E. *An Introduction to Inequalities.* Washington, DC: Mathematical Association of America, 1975.

HARDY, G.H.; LITTLEWOOD, J.E.; AND PÓLYA, GEORGE. *Inequalities,* Second Edition. New York, NY: Cambridge University Press, 1952, 1988.

KAZARINOFF, NICHOLAS D. *Analytic Inequalities.* New York, NY: Holt, Rinehart and Winston, 1961.

* OLVER, F.W.J. *Asymptotics and Special Functions.* New York, NY: Academic Press, 1974.

* ROBINSON, ABRAHAM. *Non-standard Analysis.* Amsterdam: North-Holland, 1966.

9 Foundations and Mathematical Logic

9.1 Surveys

BETH, EVERT. *The Foundations of Mathematics.* Amsterdam: North-Holland, 1959.

** EVES, HOWARD W. *Foundations and Fundamental Concepts of Mathematics,* Third Edition. Boston, MA: PWS-Kent, 1990.

MAC LANE, SAUNDERS. *Mathematics, Form and Function.* New York, NY: Springer-Verlag, 1986.

9.2 Logic

* BARWISE, JON AND ETCHEMENDY, JOHN. *The Language of First-Order Logic.* Stanford, CA: Center for Study of Language & Information, 1990.

BELL, J.L. AND MACHOVER, MOSHÉ. *A Course in Mathematical Logic.* Amsterdam: North-Holland, 1977.

* BOOLE, GEORGE. *An Investigation of the Laws of Thought.* Mineola, NY: Dover, 1951.

ENDERTON, HERBERT B. *A Mathematical Introduction to Logic.* New York, NY: Academic Press, 1972.

KLEENE, STEPHEN C. *Introduction to Metamathematics.* Amsterdam: North-Holland, 1974.

* KLEENE, STEPHEN C. *Mathematical Logic.* New York, NY: John Wiley, 1967.

KNEEBONE, G.T. *Mathematical Logic and the Foundations of Mathematics.* New York, NY: Van Nostrand Reinhold, 1963.

** LAKATOS, IMRE. *Proofs and Refutations: The Logic of Mathematical Discovery.* New York, NY: Cambridge University Press, 1976.

* MENDELSON, ELLIOTT. *Introduction to Mathematical Logic,* Third Edition. New York, NY: Van Nostrand Reinhold, 1964; Belmont, CA: Wadsworth, 1987.

** NAGEL, ERNEST AND NEWMAN, JAMES R. *Gödel's Proof.* New York, NY: New York University Press, 1958.

9.3 Set Theory

DEVLIN, KEITH J. *Fundamentals of Contemporary Set Theory.* New York, NY: Springer-Verlag, 1979.

ENDERTON, HERBERT B. *Elements of Set Theory.* New York, NY: Academic Press, 1977.

FRAENKEL, ABRAHAM A. *Abstract Set Theory,* Third Edition. Amsterdam: North Holland, 1953, 1966.

*** HALMOS, PAUL R. *Naive Set Theory.* New York, NY: Springer-Verlag, 1974.

9.4 Model Theory

CHANG, C.C. AND KEISLER, H. JEROME. *Model Theory,* Third Edition. Amsterdam: North-Holland, 1973, 1990.

HODGES, W. *Building Models by Games.* New York, NY: Cambridge University Press, 1985.

10 Discrete Mathematics

10.1 Discrete Mathematics

* ALTHOEN, STEVEN C. AND BUMCROT, ROBERT J. *Introduction to Discrete Mathematics.* Boston, MA: PWS-Kent, 1988.

DOERR, ALAN AND LEVASSEUR, KENNETH. *Applied Discrete Structures for Computer Science.* Chicago, IL: Science Research Association, 1985.

DOSSEY, JOHN A., *et al. Discrete Mathematics.* Glenview, IL: Scott Foresman, 1986.

EPP, SUSANNA S. *Discrete Mathematics with Applications.* Belmont, CA: Wadsworth, 1990.

*** GERSTEIN, LARRY J. *Discrete Mathematics and Algebraic Structures.* New York, NY: W.H. Freeman, 1987.

JOHNSONBAUGH, RICHARD. *Discrete Mathematics,* Second Edition. New York, NY: Macmillan, 1990.

* MAURER, STEPHEN B. AND RALSTON, ANTHONY. *Discrete Algorithmic Mathematics.* Reading, MA: Addison-Wesley, 1991.

POLIMENI, ALBERT D. AND STRAIGHT, H. JOSEPH. *Foundations of Discrete Mathematics,* Second Edition. Pacific Grove, CA: Brooks/Cole, 1985, 1990.

ROMAN, STEVEN. *An Introduction to Discrete Mathematics,* Second Edition. Philadelphia, PA: Saunders College, 1986; San Diego, CA: Harcourt Brace Jovanovich, 1989.

* ROSS, KENNETH A. AND WRIGHT, CHARLES R.B. *Discrete Mathematics,* Second Edition. Englewood Cliffs, NJ: Prentice Hall, 1985, 1988.

10.2 Finite Mathematics

* ANTON, HOWARD; KOLMAN, BERNARD; AND AVERBACH, BONNIE. *Applied Finite Mathematics,* Fourth Edition. New York, NY: Academic Press, 1982, 1988.

** BITTINGER, MARVIN L. AND CROWN, J. CONRAD. *Finite Mathematics.* Reading, MA: Addison-Wesley, 1989.

* GOLDSTEIN, LARRY J.; SCHNEIDER, DAVID I.; AND SIEGEL, MARTHA J. *Finite Mathematics and Its Applications,* Fourth Edition. Englewood Cliffs, NJ: Prentice Hall, 1984, 1991.

HOENIG, ALAN. *Applied Finite Mathematics.* New York, NY: McGraw-Hill, 1990.

** KEMENY, JOHN G.; SNELL, J. LAURIE; AND THOMPSON, GERALD L. *Introduction to Finite Mathematics,* Third Edition. Englewood Cliffs, NJ: Prentice Hall, 1974.

* MAKI, DANIEL P. AND THOMPSON, MAYNARD. *Finite Mathematics,* Third Edition. New York, NY: McGraw-Hill, 1978, 1989.

MALKEVITCH, JOSEPH AND MEYER, WALTER. *Graphs, Models, and Finite Mathematics.* Englewood Cliffs, NJ: Prentice Hall, 1974.

SMITH, KARL J. *Finite Mathematics,* Second Edition. Pacific Grove, CA: Brooks/Cole, 1988.

TAN, S.T. *Applied Finite Mathematics,* Third Edition. Boston, MA: Prindle, Weber and Schmidt, 1983, 1990.

10.3 Combinatorics

BOGART, KENNETH P. *Introductory Combinatorics,* Second Edition. Brooklyn, NY: Pitman, 1983; San Diego, CA: Harcourt Brace Jovanovich, 1990.

COHEN, DANIEL I.A. *Basic Techniques of Combinatorial Theory.* New York, NY: John Wiley, 1978.

* CONWAY, JOHN HORTON. *On Numbers and Games.* New York, NY: Academic Press, 1976.

DENES, J. AND KEEDWELL, A.D. *Latin Squares and Their Applications.* New York, NY: Academic Press, 1974.

** GRAHAM, RONALD L.; KNUTH, DONALD E.; AND PATASHNIK, OREN. *Concrete Mathematics: A Foundation for Computer Science.* Reading, MA: Addison-Wesley, 1989.

JACKSON, BRAD AND THORO, DMITRI. *Applied Combinatorics with Problem Solving.* Reading, MA: Addison-Wesley, 1990.

*** NIVEN, IVAN M. *Mathematics of Choice or How to Count Without Counting.* Washington, DC: Mathematical Association of America, 1975.

ROBERTS, FRED S. *Applied Combinatorics.* Englewood Cliffs, NJ: Prentice Hall, 1984.

RYSER, H.J. *Combinatorial Mathematics.* Washington, DC: Mathematical Association of America, 1963.

** TUCKER, ALAN. *Applied Combinatorics.* New York, NY: John Wiley, 1980, 1984.

10.4 Graph Theory

BARNETTE, DAVID. *Map Coloring, Polyhedra, and the Four-Color Problem.* Washington, DC: Mathematical Association of America, 1983.

BIGGS, NORMAN L.; LLOYD, E. KEITH; AND WILSON, ROBIN J. *Graph Theory, 1736–1936.* New York, NY: Clarendon Press, 1976; New York, NY: Oxford University Press, 1986.

** BONDY, J. ADRIAN AND MURTY, U.S.R. *Graph Theory with Applications.* New York, NY: American Elsevier, 1976.

BUCKLEY, FRED AND HARARY, FRANK. *Distance in Graphs.* Reading, MA: Addison-Wesley, 1990.

CHARTRAND, GARY. *Introductory Graph Theory.* (Former title: *Graphs as Mathematical Models.*) Boston, MA: Prindle, Weber and Schmidt, 1977; Mineola, NY: Dover, 1985.

HARARY, FRANK. *Graph Theory.* Reading, MA: Addison-Wesley, 1969.

*** ORE, OYSTEIN. *Graphs and Their Uses.* Washington, DC: Mathematical Association of America, 1963, 1990.

SAATY, THOMAS L. AND KAINEN, PAUL C. *The Four-Color Problem: Assaults and Conquest.* New York, NY: McGraw-Hill, 1977.

WILSON, ROBIN J. AND WATKINS, J. *Graphs: An Introductory Approach.* New York, NY: John Wiley, 1990.

10.5 Special Topics

** Goldberg, Samuel I. *Introduction to Difference Equations.* New York, NY: John Wiley, 1958; Mineola, NY: Dover, 1986.

 * Hill, Raymond. *A First Course in Coding Theory.* New York, NY: Clarendon Press, 1986.

 * Mickens, Ronald E. *Difference Equations.* New York, NY: Van Nostrand Reinhold, 1987.

** Thompson, Thomas M. *From Error-Correcting Codes Through Sphere Packings to Simple Groups.* Washington, DC: Mathematical Association of America, 1983.

11 Number Theory

11.1 Introductory Texts

Allenby, R.B.J.T. and Redfern, E.J. *Introduction to Number Theory with Computing.* New York, NY: Edward Arnold, 1989.

 * Davenport, Harold. *The Higher Arithmetic: An Introduction to the Theory of Numbers,* Fifth Edition. Atlantic Highlands, NJ: Humanities Press, 1968; New York, NY: Cambridge University Press, 1982.

Dudley, Underwood. *Elementary Number Theory,* Second Edition. New York, NY: W.H. Freeman, 1978.

 * Nagell, Trygve. *Introduction to Number Theory.* New York, NY: Chelsea, 1964.

*** Niven, Ivan M.; Zuckerman, Herbert S.; and Montgomery, Hugh L. *An Introduction to the Theory of Numbers,* Fifth Edition. New York, NY: John Wiley, 1966, 1991.

11.2 Expositions

Khinchin, A. Ya. *Three Pearls of Number Theory.* Baltimore, MD: Graylock Press, 1952.

 * Niven, Ivan M. *Irrational Numbers.* Washington, DC: Mathematical Association of America, 1959.

*** Niven, Ivan M. *Numbers: Rational and Irrational.* Washington, DC: Mathematical Association of America, 1961.

Ogilvy, C. Stanley and Anderson, John T. *Excursions in Number Theory.* New York, NY: Oxford University Press, 1966.

** Ore, Oystein. *Invitation to Number Theory.* Washington, DC: Mathematical Association of America, 1967, 1975.

Schroeder, Manfred R. *Number Theory in Science and Communication with Applications in Cryptography, Physics, Digital Information, Computing, and Self-Similarity,* Second Enlarged Edition. New York, NY: Springer-Verlag, 1984, 1986.

 * Weil, André. *Number Theory: An Approach Through History From Hammurapi to Legendre.* New York, NY: Birkhäuser, 1984.

11.3 Elementary Monographs

Davis, Philip J. *The Lore of Large Numbers.* Washington, DC: Mathematical Association of America, 1975.

** Guy, Richard K. *Unsolved Problems in Number Theory.* New York, NY: Springer-Verlag, 1981.

 * Hardy, G.H. and Wright, E.M. *Introduction to the Theory of Numbers,* Fifth Edition. New York, NY: Oxford University Press, 1960, 1979.

LeVeque, William J. *Topics in Number Theory,* 2 Vols. Reading, MA: Addison-Wesley, 1956.

 * Olds, C.D. *Continued Fractions.* Washington, DC: Mathematical Association of America, 1963.

** Ore, Oystein. *Number Theory and Its History.* Mineola, NY: Dover, 1988.

 * Sierpiński, W. *250 Problems in Elementary Number Theory.* New York, NY: American Elsevier, 1970.

Vorob'ev, N.N. *Fibonacci Numbers.* New York, NY: Blaisdell, 1961.

11.4 Primes and Factors

BRESSOUD, DAVID M. *Factorization and Primality Testing.* New York, NY: Springer-Verlag, 1989.

POMERANCE, CARL. *Lecture Notes on Primality Testing and Factoring: A Short Course at Kent State University.* Washington, DC: Mathematical Association of America, 1984.

RIBENBOIM, PAULO. *The Book of Prime Number Records,* Second Edition. New York, NY: Springer-Verlag, 1988, 1989.

** RIBENBOIM, PAULO. *The Little Book of Big Primes.* New York, NY: Springer-Verlag, 1991.

11.5 Algebraic Number Theory

EDWARDS, HAROLD M. *Fermat's Last Theorem: A Genetic Introduction to Algebraic Number Theory.* New York, NY: Springer-Verlag, 1977.

* POLLARD, HARRY AND DIAMOND, H.G. *The Theory of Algebraic Numbers,* Second Edition. Washington, DC: Mathematical Association of America, 1976.

STEWART, IAN AND TALL, DAVID. *Algebraic Number Theory,* Second Edition. New York, NY: Chapman and Hall, 1979, 1987.

12 Linear Algebra

12.1 Elementary

** ANTON, HOWARD. *Elementary Linear Algebra,* Sixth Edition. New York, NY: John Wiley, 1973, 1991.

BANCHOFF, THOMAS F. AND WERMER, JOHN. *Linear Algebra Through Geometry.* New York, NY: Springer-Verlag, 1983.

FRALEIGH, JOHN B. AND BEAUREGARD, RAYMOND A. *Linear Algebra,* Second Edition. Reading, MA: Addison-Wesley, 1990.

KUMPEL, P.G. AND THORPE, JOHN A. *Linear Algebra with Applications to Differential Equations.* Philadelphia, PA: Saunders College, 1983.

* LANG, SERGE. *Introduction to Linear Algebra,* Second Edition. New York, NY: Springer-Verlag, 1986.

LIPSCHUTZ, SEYMOUR. *Schaum's Solved Problems Series: 3000 Solved Problems in Linear Algebra.* New York, NY: McGraw-Hill, 1989.

NOBLE, BEN AND DANIEL, JAMES W. *Applied Linear Algebra,* Third Edition. Englewood Cliffs, NJ: Prentice Hall, 1969, 1988.

O'NAN, MICHAEL AND ENDERTON, HERBERT B. *Linear Algebra,* Third Edition. San Diego, CA: Harcourt Brace Jovanovich, 1990.

RORRES, CHRIS AND ANTON, HOWARD. *Applications of Linear Algebra,* Third Edition. New York, NY: John Wiley, 1977, 1984.

SMITH, LARRY. *Linear Algebra.* New York, NY: Springer-Verlag, 1978.

** STRANG, GILBERT. *Linear Algebra and Its Applications,* Third Edition. New York, NY: Academic Press, 1976; San Diego, CA: Harcourt Brace Jovanovich, 1988.

* TUCKER, ALAN. *A Unified Introduction to Linear Algebra: Models, Methods, and Theory.* New York, NY: Macmillan, 1988. vglue -4pt

12.2 Advanced

* HALMOS, PAUL R. *Finite-Dimensional Vector Spaces.* New York, NY: Springer-Verlag, 1968, 1974.

* HOFFMAN, KENNETH AND KUNZE, RAY. *Linear Algebra,* Second Edition. Englewood Cliffs, NJ: Prentice Hall, 1971.

LANG, SERGE. *Linear Algebra,* Third Edition. New York, NY: Springer-Verlag, 1987.

13 Algebra

13.1 Introductory Surveys

BARBEAU, EDWARD J. *Polynomials.* New York, NY: Springer-Verlag, 1989.

*** BIRKHOFF, GARRETT AND MAC LANE, SAUNDERS. *A Survey of Modern Algebra,* Fourth Edition. New York, NY: Macmillan, 1965, 1977.

* CHILDS, LINDSAY. *A Concrete Introduction to Higher Algebra.* New York, NY: Springer-Verlag, 1979.

DORNHOFF, LARRY L. AND HOHN, FRANZ E. *Applied Modern Algebra.* New York, NY: Macmillan, 1978.

* GALLIAN, JOSEPH A. *Contemporary Abstract Algebra,* Second Edition. Lexington, MA: D.C. Heath, 1986, 1990.

** HERSTEIN, I.N. *Abstract Algebra,* Second Edition. New York, NY: Macmillan, 1986, 1990.

* HILLMAN, ABRAHAM P. AND ALEXANDERSON, GERALD L. *A First Undergraduate Course in Abstract Algebra,* Fourth Edition. Belmont, CA: Wadsworth, 1973, 1988.

HUNGERFORD, THOMAS W. *Abstract Algebra: An Introduction.* Philadelphia, PA: Saunders College, 1990.

McCOY, NEAL H. AND JANUSZ, GERALD J. *Introduction to Modern Algebra,* Fourth Edition. Boston, MA: Allyn and Bacon, 1960, 1987.

PINTER, CHARLES C. *A Book of Abstract Algebra.* New York, NY: McGraw-Hill, 1982.

13.2 Advanced Surveys

HALMOS, PAUL R. *Lectures on Boolean Algebras.* New York, NY: Springer-Verlag, 1974.

* HERSTEIN, I.N. *Topics in Algebra,* Second Edition. New York, NY: John Wiley, 1975.

LANG, SERGE. *Algebra,* Second Edition. Reading, MA: Addison-Wesley, 1965, 1984.

MAC LANE, SAUNDERS AND BIRKHOFF, GARRETT. *Algebra,* Third Edition. New York, NY: Macmillan, 1967; New York, NY: Chelsea, 1988.

* VAN DER WAERDEN, B.L. *Algebra,* 2 Vols., Seventh Edition. (Original title: *Modern Algebra.*) New York, NY: Frederick Ungar, 1950; New York, NY: Springer-Verlag, 1991.

13.3 Group Theory

** BUDDEN, F.J. *The Fascination of Groups.* New York, NY: Cambridge University Press, 1972.

BURN, R.P. *Groups: A Path to Geometry.* New York, NY: Cambridge University Press, 1985, 1987.

** HALL, MARSHALL, JR. *The Theory of Groups,* Second Edition. New York, NY: Macmillan, 1959; New York, NY: Chelsea, 1973.

* ROTMAN, JOSEPH J. *An Introduction to the Theory of Groups,* Third Edition. Needham Heights, MA: Allyn and Bacon, 1965, 1984.

13.4 Rings and Ideals

KAPLANSKY, IRVING. *Fields and Rings,* Revised Second Edition. Chicago, IL: University of Chicago Press, 1969, 1974.

McCOY, NEAL H. *Rings and Ideals.* Washington, DC: Mathematical Association of America, 1948.

McCOY, NEAL H. *The Theory of Rings.* New York, NY: Macmillan, 1964; New York, NY: Chelsea, 1973.

ROBINSON, ABRAHAM. *Numbers and Ideals.* San Francisco, CA: Holden-Day, 1965.

* SHARPE, DAVID. *Rings and Factorization.* New York, NY: Cambridge University Press, 1987.

13.5 Fields and Galois Theory

ARTIN, EMIL. *Galois Theory*, Second Revised Edition. Notre Dame, IN: University of Notre Dame Press, 1966.

GAAL, LISL. *Classical Galois Theory with Examples*, Fourth Edition. Boston, MA: Markham, 1971; New York, NY: Chelsea, 1973, 1988.

** HADLOCK, CHARLES R. *Field Theory and Its Classical Problems.* Washington, DC: Mathematical Association of America, 1978.

** LIEBER, LILLIAN R. *Galois and the Theory of Groups: A Bright Star in Mathesis.* Brooklyn, NY: Galois Institute of Mathematics and Art, 1961.

13.6 Commutative Algebra

* ATIYAH, MICHAEL F. AND MACDONALD, I.G. *Introduction to Commutative Algebra.* Reading, MA: Addison-Wesley, 1969.

KAPLANSKY, IRVING. *Commutative Rings,* Revised Edition. Chicago, IL: University of Chicago Press, 1974; Boston, MA: Allyn and Bacon, 1974.

ZARISKI, OSCAR AND SAMUEL, PIERRE. *Commutative Algebra,* 2 Vols. New York, NY: Springer-Verlag, 1975, 1976.

14 Geometry

14.1 General

*** BANCHOFF, THOMAS F. *Beyond the Third Dimension: Geometry, Computer Graphics, and Higher Dimensions.* New York, NY: Scientific American Library, 1990.

BOLD, BENJAMIN. *Famous Problems of Geometry and How to Solve Them.* New York, NY: Van Nostrand Reinhold, 1969; Mineola, NY: Dover, 1982.

BURGER, DIONYS. *Sphereland.* New York, NY: Thomas Y. Crowell, 1965.

** HILBERT, DAVID AND COHN-VOSSEN, S. *Geometry and the Imagination.* New York, NY: Chelsea, 1952.

* HILDEBRANDT, STEFAN AND TROMBA, ANTHONY J. *Mathematics and Optimal Form.* New York, NY: Scientific American Library, 1984.

** KRAUSE, EUGENE F. *Taxicab Geometry: An Adventure in Non-Euclidean Geometry.* Reading, MA: Addison-Wesley, 1975; Mineola, NY: Dover, 1986.

* RUCKER, RUDY. *Geometry, Relativity, and the Fourth Dimension.* Mineola, NY: Dover, 1977.

14.2 Surveys

CEDERBERG, JUDITH N. *A Course in Modern Geometries.* New York, NY: Springer-Verlag, 1989.

*** COXETER, H.S.M. *Introduction to Geometry,* Second Edition. New York, NY: John Wiley, 1969.

** EVES, HOWARD W. *A Survey of Geometry,* Second Revised Edition. Boston, MA: Allyn and Bacon, 1972.

* PEDOE, DAN. *Geometry and the Visual Arts.* (Former title: *Geometry and the Liberal Arts.*) New York, NY: St. Martin's Press, 1978; Mineola, NY: Dover, 1983.

SMART, JAMES R. *Modern Geometries,* Third Edition. Pacific Grove, CA: Brooks/Cole, 1973, 1988.

* STEHNEY, ANN K., et al., EDS. *Selected Papers on Geometry.* Washington, DC: Mathematical Association of America, 1979.

14.3 School Geometry

HOFFER, ALAN. *Geometry.* Reading, MA: Addison-Wesley, 1979.

* JACOBS, HAROLD R. *Geometry*, Second Edition. New York, NY: W.H. Freeman, 1974, 1986.

KEMPE, A.B. *How to Draw a Straight Line.* Reston, VA: National Council of Teachers of Mathematics, 1977.

LOOMIS, E. *The Pythagorean Proposition.* Reston, VA: National Council of Teachers of Mathematics, 1968.

MOISE, EDWIN E. AND DOWNS, FLOYD L. *Geometry.* Reading, MA: Addison-Wesley, 1975.

** O'DAFFER, PHARES G. AND CLEMENS, STANLEY R. *Geometry: An Investigative Approach.* Reading, MA: Addison-Wesley, 1976.

14.4 Euclidean and Non-Euclidean Geometry

* COXETER, H.S.M., *et al. Geometry Revisited.* Washington, DC: Mathematical Association of America, 1967.

** DUDLEY, UNDERWOOD. *A Budget of Trisections.* New York, NY: Springer-Verlag, 1987.

GREENBERG, MARVIN JAY. *Euclidean and Non-Euclidean Geometries: Development and History.* New York, NY: W.H. Freeman, 1974, 1980.

PEDOE, DAN. *Circles: A Mathematical View.* Mineola, NY: Dover, 1979.

* YATES, ROBERT C. *The Trisection Problem.* Reston, VA: National Council of Teachers of Mathematics, 1971.

14.5 Polyhedra, Tilings, Symmetry

COXETER, H.S.M., *et al.*, EDS. *M.C. Escher: Art and Science.* New York, NY: Elsevier Science, 1986.

** GRÜNBAUM, BRANKO AND SHEPHARD, G.C. *Tilings and Patterns.* New York, NY: W.H. Freeman, 1986, 1989.

* HILTON, PETER J. AND PEDERSEN, JEAN. *Build Your Own Polyhedra.* Reading, MA: Addison-Wesley, 1988.

HOLDEN, ALAN. *Orderly Tangles: Cloverleafs, Gordian Knots, and Regular Polylinks.* New York, NY: Columbia University Press, 1983.

LOCKWOOD, E.H. AND MACMILLAN, R.H. *Geometric Symmetry.* New York, NY: Cambridge University Press, 1978.

MacGILLAVRY, CAROLINE H. *Fantasy & Symmetry: The Periodic Drawings of M.S. Escher.* New York, NY: Harry N. Abrams, 1976.

PUGH, ANTHONY. *Polyhedra: A Visual Approach.* Berkeley, CA: University of California Press, 1976.

RANUCCI, E.R. AND TEETERS, J.L. *Creating Escher-Type Drawings.* Palo Alto, CA: Creative Publ., 1977.

*** SCHATTSCHNEIDER, DORIS J. *Visions of Symmetry: Notebooks, Periodic Drawings, and Related Work of M.C. Escher.* New York, NY: W.H. Freeman, 1990.

* SENECHAL, MARJORIE AND FLECK, GEORGE, EDS. *Shaping Space: A Polyhedral Approach.* New York, NY: Birkhäuser, 1988.

WENNINGER, MAGNUS J. *Spherical Models.* New York, NY: Cambridge University Press, 1979.

14.6 Computational Geometry

* ABELSON, HAROLD AND diSESSA, ANDREA A. *Turtle Geometry: The Computer as a Medium for Exploring Mathematics.* Cambridge, MA: MIT Press, 1981.

BILLSTEIN, RICK; LIBESKIND, S.; AND LOTT, JOHNNY W. *Logo.* Redwood City, CA: Benjamin Cummings, 1985.

CLAYSON, J. *Visual Modeling with Logo.* Cambridge, MA: MIT Press, 1988.

O'ROURKE, JOSEPH. *Art Gallery Theorems and Algorithms.* New York, NY: Oxford University Press, 1987.

14.7 Algebraic and Differential Geometry

BRIESKORN, EGBERT AND KNÖRRER, HORST. *Plane Algebraic Curves.* New York, NY: Birkhäuser, 1986.

FULTON, WILLIAM. *Algebraic Curves: An Introduction to Algebraic Geometry.* Reading, MA: W.A. Benjamin, 1969.

O'NEILL, BARRETT. *Elementary Differential Geometry.* New York, NY: Academic Press, 1966.

SEIDENBERG, A., ED. *Studies in Algebraic Geometry.* Washington, DC: Mathematical Association of America, 1980.

14.8 Special Topics

BAKEL'MAN, I. YA. *Inversions.* Chicago, IL: University of Chicago Press, 1974.

* BLUMENTHAL, LEONARD M. *Modern View of Geometry.* New York, NY: W.H. Freeman, 1961; Mineola, NY: Dover, 1980.

LOCKWOOD, E.H. *A Book of Curves.* New York, NY: Cambridge University Press, 1960.

LYUSTERNIK, L.A. *The Shortest Lines: Variational Problems.* Moscow: MIR, 1976, 1983.

** YAGLOM, I.M. *Geometric Transformations,* 3 Vols. Washington, DC: Mathematical Association of America, 1962–73.

* YATES, ROBERT C. *Curves and Their Properties.* Reston, VA: National Council of Teachers of Mathematics, 1974.

YOUNG, JOHN WESLEY. *Projective Geometry.* Washington, DC: Mathematical Association of America, 1930.

15 Topology

15.1 General Topology

* ALEXANDROFF, PAUL. *Elementary Concepts of Topology.* Mineola, NY: Dover, 1961.

** BING, R.H. *Elementary Point Set Topology.* Washington, DC: Mathematical Association of America, 1960.

*** CHINN, WILLIAM G. AND STEENROD, NORMAN E. *First Concepts of Topology.* Washington, DC: Mathematical Association of America, 1966.

KELLEY, JOHN L. *General Topology,* New York, NY: Van Nostrand Reinhold, 1955; New York, NY: Springer-Verlag, 1975.

MUNKRES, JAMES R. *Topology: A First Course.* Englewood Cliffs, NJ: Prentice Hall, 1975.

* SIMMONS, GEORGE F. *Introduction to Topology and Modern Analysis.* New York, NY: McGraw-Hill, 1963; Melbourne, FL: Robert E. Krieger, 1983.

* STEEN, LYNN ARTHUR AND SEEBACH, J. ARTHUR, JR. *Counterexamples in Topology,* Second Edition. New York, NY: Holt, Rinehart and Winston, 1970; New York, NY: Springer-Verlag, 1978.

** WILLARD, STEPHEN. *General Topology.* Reading, MA: Addison-Wesley, 1970.

15.2 Geometric Topology

** FIRBY, P.A. AND GARDINER, C.F. *Surface Topology.* New York, NY: Halsted Press, 1982; New York, NY: Ellis Horwood, 1982.

FRANCIS, GEORGE K. *A Topological Picturebook.* New York, NY: Springer-Verlag, 1987.

ROLFSEN, DALE. *Knots and Links,* Second Edition. Boston, MA: Publish or Perish, 1976, 1991.

* WEEKS, JEFFREY R. *The Shape of Space: How to Visualize Surfaces and Three-Dimensional Manifolds.* New York, NY: Marcel Dekker, 1985.

15.3 Algebraic Topology

GIBLIN, P.J. *Graphs, Surfaces and Homology: An Introduction to Algebraic Topology*, Second Edition. New York, NY: Halsted Press, 1977; New York, NY: Chapman and Hall, 1981.

GREENBERG, MARVIN JAY AND HARPER, JOHN R. *Lectures on Algebraic Topology*, Second Edition. Reading, MA: W.A. Benjamin, 1967, 1981.

* HENLE, MICHAEL. *A Combinatorial Introduction to Topology.* New York, NY: W.H. Freeman, 1979.

* MASSEY, WILLIAM S. *Algebraic Topology: An Introduction.* San Diego, CA: Harcourt Brace Jovanovich, 1967; New York, NY: Springer-Verlag, 1977.

15.4 Differential Topology

MILNOR, JOHN W. *Topology from the Differentiable Viewpoint.* Charlottesville, VA: University Press of Virginia, 1965.

* SINGER, I.M. AND THORPE, JOHN A. *Lecture Notes on Elementary Topology and Geometry.* Glenview, IL: Scott Foresman, 1967; New York, NY: Springer-Verlag, 1987.

16 Vocational and Technical Mathematics

16.1 Industrial Mathematics

** AUSTIN, JACQUELINE C.; GILL, JACK C.; AND ISERN, MARGARITA. *Technical Mathematics*, Fourth Edition. Philadelphia, PA: Saunders College, 1988.

CLEAVES, CHERYL; HOBBS, MARGIE; AND DUDENHEFER, PAUL. *Introduction to Technical Mathematics.* Englewood Cliffs, NJ: Prentice Hall, 1988.

*** EWEN, DALE AND NELSON, C. ROBERT. *Elementary Technical Mathematics*, Fifth Edition. Belmont, CA: Wadsworth, 1978, 1991.

KUHFITTIG, PETER K.F. *Introduction to Technical Mathematics.* Pacific Grove, CA: Brooks/Cole, 1986.

LEFFIN, WALTER W., *et al. Introduction to Technical Mathematics.* Prospect Heights, IL: Waveland, 1987.

LYNG, M.J., *et al. Applied Technical Mathematics*, Revised Edition. Boston, MA: Houghton Mifflin, 1978; Prospect Heights, IL: Waveland, 1983.

* MCHALE, THOMAS J. AND WITZKE, PAUL T. *Technical Mathematics I and II.* Reading, MA: Addison-Wesley, 1988.

MOORE, CLAUDE S., *et al. Applied Math for Technicians*, Second Edition. Englewood Cliffs, NJ: Prentice Hall, 1982.

NUSTAD, HARRY L. AND WESNER, TERRY H. *Essentials of Technical Mathematics.* Dubuque, IA: William C. Brown, 1984.

PAUL, RICHARD S. AND SHAEVEL, M. LEONARD. *Essentials of Technical Mathematics*, Second Edition. Englewood Cliffs, NJ: Prentice Hall, 1982.

* SMITH, ROBERT D. *Vocational-Technical Mathematics*, Second Edition. Albany, NY: Delmar, 1983, 1991.

WALL, CHARLES R. *Basic Technical Mathematics.* San Diego, CA: Harcourt Brace Jovanovich, 1986.

* WASHINGTON, ALLYN J. AND TRIOLA, MARIO F. *Introduction to Technical Mathematics*, Fourth Edition. Redwood City, CA: Benjamin Cummings, 1988.

16.2 Mathematics for Trades

ANDERSON, J.G. *Technical Shop Mathematics*, Second Edition. New York, NY: Industrial Press, 1974, 1983.

BALL, JOHN E. *Practical Problems in Mathematics for Masons.* Albany, NY: Delmar, 1980.

* Boyce, John B., *et al. Mathematics for Technical and Vocational Students,* Eighth Edition. New York, NY: John Wiley, 1989.

Bradford, Robert. *Mathematics for Carpenters.* Albany, NY: Delmar, 1975.

Carlo, Patrick and Murphy, Dennis. *Merchandising Mathematics,* Second Edition. Albany, NY: Delmar, 1981.

Carman, Robert A. and Saunders, Hal M. *Mathematics for the Trades: A Guided Approach,* Second Edition. New York, NY: John Wiley, 1986.

* Cleaves, Cheryl, *et al. Basic Mathematics for Trades and Technologies,* Second Edition. Englewood Cliffs, NJ: Prentice Hall, 1990.

* DeVore, Russell. *Practical Problems in Mathematics for Heating and Cooling Technicians.* Albany, NY: Delmar, 1981.

Felker, C.A. and Bradley, J.G. *Shop Mathematics,* Sixth Edition. New York, NY: McGraw-Hill, 1976, 1984.

* Garrad, Crawford G. and Herman, Stephen L. *Practical Problems in Mathematics for Electricians,* Fourth Edition. Albany, NY: Delmar, 1987.

Goetsch, David L., *et al. Mathematics for the Automotive Trades.* Englewood Cliffs, NJ: Prentice Hall, 1988.

Goetsch, David L., *et al. Mathematics for the Heating, Ventilating, and Cooling Trades.* Englewood Cliffs, NJ: Prentice Hall, 1988.

Goetsch, David L., *et al. Mathematics for the Machine Trades.* Englewood Cliffs, NJ: Prentice Hall, 1988.

Goritz, John. *Mathematics for Welding Trades.* Englewood Cliffs, NJ: Prentice Hall, 1987.

* Guest, Russell J., *et al. Mathematics for Plumbers and Pipe Fitters,* Fourth Edition. Albany, NY: Delmar, 1990.

Haines, Robert G. *Math Principles for Food Service Occupations,* Second Edition. Albany, NY: Delmar, 1988.

* Hendrix, T.G. and LeFevor, C.S. *Mathematics for Auto Mechanics.* Albany, NY: Delmar, 1978.

Hoffman, Edward G. and Davis, Dennis D. *Practical Problems in Mathematics for Machinists,* Third Edition. Albany, NY: Delmar, 1988.

Huth, H. *Practical Problems in Mathematics for Carpenters,* Fifth Edition. Albany, NY: Delmar, 1955, 1991.

McMackin, Frank J., *et al. Mathematics of the Shop,* Fourth Edition. Albany, NY: Delmar, 1978.

* Moore, George. *Practical Problems in Mathematics for Automotive Technicians,* Third Edition. Albany, NY: Delmar, 1984.

** Oberg, Eric, *et al. Machinery's Handbook,* Twenty-Third Edition. New York, NY: Industrial Press, 1975, 1988.

Olivo, C. Thomas and Olivo, Thomas P. *Basic Vocational-Technical Mathematics,* Fifth Edition. Albany, NY: Delmar, 1985.

Palmer, Claude I. and Mrachek, Leonard A. *Practical Mathematics,* Seventh Edition. New York, NY: McGraw-Hill, 1986.

Peterson, John C. and deKryger, William J. *Math for the Automotive Trade,* Second Edition. Albany, NY: Delmar, 1989.

* Schell, Frank R. and Matlock, Bill J. *Practical Problems in Mathematics for Welders,* Third Edition. Albany, NY: Delmar, 1988.

*** Smith, Robert D. *Mathematics for Machine Technology,* Third Edition. Albany, NY: Delmar, 1990.

Vermeersch, LaVonne F. and Southwick, Charles E. *Practical Problems in Mathematics for Graphic Arts.* Albany, NY: Delmar, 1982.

* Wolfe, John H. and Phelps, E.R. *Practical Shop Mathematics,* Fourth Edition. New York, NY: McGraw-Hill, 1958.

16.3 Health Sciences

BATASTINI, PEGGY H. AND DAVIDSON, JUDY K. *Pharmacological Calculations for Nurses: A Worktext.* Albany, NY: Delmar, 1985.

CAROLAN, MARY JANE. *Clinical Calculations for Nurses.* East Norwalk, CT: Appleton and Lange, 1990.

DANIELS, JEANNE M. AND SMITH, LORETTA M. *Clinical Calculations: A Unified Approach.* Albany, NY: Delmar, 1986.

*** HAYDEN, JEROME D. AND DAVIS, HOWARD T. *Fundamental Mathematics for Health Careers,* Second Edition. Albany, NY: Delmar, 1980, 1990.

HIGHERS, MICHAEL P. AND FORRESTER, ROBERT P. *Mathematics for the Allied Health Professions.* East Norwalk, CT: Appleton and Lange, 1987.

** HOIT, LAURA K. *The Arithmetic of Dosages and Solutions,* Seventh Edition. St. Louis, MO: Mosby and Company, 1989.

KEE, JOYCE L. AND MARSHAL, SALLY M. *Clinical Calculations with Applications to General and Specialty Areas.* Philadelphia, PA: Saunders College, 1988.

* MIDICI, GERALDINE ANN. *Drug Dosage Calculations: A Guide to Clinical Calculation.* East Norwalk, CT: Appleton and Lange, 1988.

MOORE, SUSAN G.; HOWLAND, JOSEPH W.; AND SAVAGE, KATHERINE. *Nursing Simplified: Math Logic.* Clearwater, FL: H and H Publishers, 1986.

** PICKAR, GLORIA D. *Dosage Calculations,* Third Edition. Albany, NY: Delmar, 1987, 1990.

RICE, JANE AND SKELLEY, ESTHER G. *Medications and Mathematics for the Nurse,* Sixth Edition. Albany, NY: Delmar, 1988.

* RICHARDSON, JUDITH K. AND RICHARDSON, LLOYD I. *The Mathematics of Drugs and Solutions with Clinical Applications.* St. Louis, MO: Mosby and Company, 1990.

ROBERTS, KEITH AND MICHELS, LEO. *Mathematics for Health Sciences.* Belmont, CA: Wadsworth, 1982.

WEAVER, MABEL E. AND KOEHLER, VERA J. *Programmed Mathematics of Drugs and Solutions,* Revised Edition. Philadelphia, PA: J.B. Lippincott, 1984.

WILSON, BRUCE. *Logical Nursing Mathematics.* Albany, NY: Delmar, 1987.

16.4 Data Processing

BLISS, ELIZABETH. *Data Processing Mathematics.* Englewood Cliffs, NJ: Prentice Hall, 1985.

CALTER, PAUL. *Mathematics for Computer Technology.* Englewood Cliffs, NJ: Prentice Hall, 1986.

** CLARK, FRANK J. *Mathematics for Programming Computers,* Third Edition. Englewood Cliffs, NJ: Prentice Hall, 1988.

DEITEL, HARVEY M. AND DEITEL, BARBARA. *Computers and Data Processing.* New York, NY: Academic Press, 1985.

KOLATIS, MARIA S. *Mathematics for Data Processing and Computing.* Reading, MA: Addison-Wesley, 1985.

MCCULLOUGH, ROBERT N. *Mathematics for Data Processing.* Dubuque, IA: William C. Brown, 1988.

* NINESTEIN, ELEANOR H. *Introduction to Computer Mathematics.* Glenview, IL: Scott Foresman, 1987.

16.5 Electronics

BARKER, FORREST. *Problems in Technical Mathematics for Electricity/Electronics.* Redwood City, CA: Benjamin Cummings, 1976.

** COOKE, NELSON M.; ADAMS, HERBERT F.R.; AND DELL, PETER B. *Basic Mathematics for Electronics,* Sixth Edition. New York, NY: McGraw-Hill, 1987.

GROB, BERNARD. *Mathematics for Basic Electronics,* Third Edition. New York, NY: McGraw-Hill, 1989.

PASAHOW, EDWARD. *Mathematics for Electronics.* Albany, NY: Delmar, 1984.

POWER, THOMAS C. *Electronics Mathematics.* Albany, NY: Delmar, 1985.

RADER, CARL. *Fundamentals of Electronics Mathematics.* Albany, NY: Delmar, 1985.

RICHMOND, A.E. AND HECHT, G.W. *Calculus for Electronics,* Fourth Edition. New York, NY: McGraw-Hill, 1989.

*** SINGER, B.B. AND FORSTER, H. *Basic Mathematics for Electricity and Electronics,* Sixth Edition. New York, NY: McGraw-Hill, 1976, 1989.

SULLIVAN, RICHARD L. *Modern Electronics Mathematics.* Albany, NY: Delmar, 1985.

** SULLIVAN, RICHARD L. *Practical Problems in Mathematics for Electronics Technicians,* Second Edition. Albany, NY: Delmar, 1982, 1990.

16.6 Chemical Technology

BARD, ALLEN J. *Chemical Equilibrium.* New York, NY: Harper and Row, 1966.

** GOLDFISH, DOROTHY M. *Basic Mathematics for Beginning Chemistry,* Fourth Edition. New York, NY: Macmillan, 1990.

* HAMILTON, L.F., *et al. Calculations of Analytic Chemistry,* Seventh Edition. New York, NY: McGraw-Hill, 1969.

MARGOLIS, EMIL J. *Chemical Principles in Calculations of Tonic Equilibria.* New York, NY: Macmillan, 1966.

NYMAN, CARL J. AND KING, G. BROOKS. *Problems for General Chemistry and Qualitative Analysis,* Fourth Edition. New York, NY: John Wiley, 1975, 1980.

PETERS, M.S. *Elementary Chemical Engineering,* Second Edition. New York, NY: McGraw-Hill, 1954, 1984.

ROBBINS, OMER, JR. *Tonic Reactions and Equilibria.* New York, NY: Macmillan, 1967.

16.7 Engineering Technology

** CALTER, PAUL. *Technical Mathematics with Calculus,* Second Edition. Englewood Cliffs, NJ: Prentice Hall, 1984, 1990.

* COOKE, NELSON M.; ADAMS, HERBERT F.R.; AND DELL, PETER B. *Basic Mathematics for Electronics with Calculus.* New York, NY: McGraw-Hill, 1989.

DAVIS, LINDA. *Technical Mathematics with Calculus.* Columbus, OH: Charles E. Merrill, 1990.

EARLE, JAMES. *Geometry for Engineers.* Reading, MA: Addison-Wesley, 1984.

ELLIS, A.J. *Basic Algebra and Geometry for Scientists and Engineers.* New York, NY: John Wiley, 1982.

* EWEN, DALE AND TOPPER, MICHAEL A. *Mathematics for Technical Education,* Second Edition. Englewood Cliffs, NJ: Prentice Hall, 1983.

* EWEN, DALE AND TOPPER, MICHAEL A. *Technical Calculus,* Second Edition. Englewood Cliffs, NJ: Prentice Hall, 1986.

GOODSON, C.E. AND MIERTSCHIN, S.L. *Technical Mathematics with Calculus.* New York, NY: John Wiley, 1985.

** KRAMER, ARTHUR D. *Fundamentals of Technical Mathematics with Calculus,* Second Edition. New York, NY: McGraw-Hill, 1989.

* KUHFITTIG, PETER K.F. *Basic Technical Mathematics with Calculus,* Second Edition. Pacific Grove, CA: Brooks/Cole, 1984, 1989.

PORTER, STUART R. AND ERNST, JOHN F. *Basic Technical Mathematics with Calculus.* Reading, MA: Addison-Wesley, 1985.

RICE, HAROLD S. AND KNIGHT, RAYMOND M. *Technical Mathematics with Calculus,* Third Edition. New York, NY: McGraw-Hill, 1974.

*** WASHINGTON, ALLYN J. *Basic Technical Mathematics with Calculus,* Fifth Edition. Redwood City, CA: Benjamin Cummings, 1978, 1990.

17 Business Mathematics

17.1 Basic Skills

* BERSTON, HYMAN M. AND FISHER, PAUL. *Collegiate Business Mathematics*, Fifth Edition. Homewood, IL: Richard D. Irwin, 1990.

** BITTINGER, MARVIN L. AND RUDOLPH, WILLIAM B. *Business Mathematics for College Students*. Reading, MA: Addison-Wesley, 1986.

* BOISSELLE, A.H.; FREEMAN, D.M.; AND BRENNA, L.V. *Business Mathematics Today*. New York, NY: McGraw-Hill, 1990.

LANGE, W.H.; ROUSOS, T.G.; AND MASON, R.D. *Mathematics for Business and New Consumers*. Homewood, IL: Richard D. Irwin, 1988.

* SLATER, JEFFREY. *Practical Business Math Procedures*. Homewood, IL: Richard D. Irwin, 1987.

17.2 Algebra and Finite Mathematics

BARNETT, RAYMOND A. AND ZIEGLER, MICHAEL R. *Finite Mathematics for Management, Life, and Social Sciences*, Fourth Edition. San Francisco, CA: Dellen, 1981, 1987.

*** BARNETT, RAYMOND A.; BURKE, CHARLES J.; AND ZIEGLER, MICHAEL R. *Applied Mathematics for Business, Economics, Life Sciences, and Social Sciences*, Third Edition. San Francisco, CA: Dellen, 1989.

BEATTY, WILLIAM E. *Mathematical Relationships in Business and Economics*. Boston, MA: Prindle, Weber and Schmidt, 1970.

BUDNICK, FRANK S. *Applied Mathematics for Business, Economics, and the Social Sciences*, Third Edition. New York, NY: McGraw-Hill, 1988.

FARLOW, STANLEY J. AND HAGGARD, GARY M. *Applied Mathematics for Business, Economics, and the Social Sciences*. New York, NY: McGraw-Hill, 1988.

MIZRAHI, ABE AND SULLIVAN, MICHAEL. *Finite Mathematics with Applications for Business and Social Sciences*, Fifth Edition. New York, NY: John Wiley, 1983, 1988.

* NIEVERGELT, YVES. *Mathematics in Business Administration*. Homewood, IL: Richard D. Irwin, 1989.

SPENCE, LAWRENCE E.; VANDEN EYNDEN, CHARLES; AND GALLIN, DANIEL. *Applied Mathematics for the Management, Life, and Social Sciences*. Glenview, IL: Scott Foresman, 1990.

** STANCL, DONALD L. AND STANCL, MILDRED L. *Mathematics for the Management and the Life and Social Sciences*. Homewood, IL: Richard D. Irwin, 1990.

17.3 Business Statistics

HOSSACK, I.B.; POLLARD, J.H.; AND ZEHNWIRTH, B. *Introductory Statistics with Applications in General Insurance*. New York, NY: Cambridge University Press, 1983.

MENDENHALL, WILLIAM AND McCLAVE, JAMES T. *A Second Course in Business Statistics: Regression Analysis*, Third Edition. San Francisco, CA: Dellen, 1981, 1989.

MILLER, ROBERT B. AND WICHERN, DEAN W. *Intermediate Business Statistics*. New York, NY: Holt, Rinehart and Winston, 1977.

* NEWBOLD, PAUL. *Statistics for Business and Economics*, Second Edition. Englewood Cliffs, NJ: Prentice Hall, 1988.

*** TANUR, JUDITH M., et al., EDS. *Statistics: A Guide to Business and Economics*. San Francisco, CA: Holden-Day, 1976.

17.4 Business Calculus

BERKEY, DENNIS D. *Calculus for Management, Social, and Life Sciences*, Second Edition. Philadelphia, PA: Saunders College, 1990.

** BITTINGER, MARVIN L. AND CROWN, J. CONRAD. *Mathematics and Calculus with Applications.* Reading, MA: Addison-Wesley, 1989.

BITTINGER, MARVIN L. AND MORREL, BERNARD B. *Applied Calculus,* Second Edition. Reading, MA: Addison-Wesley, 1988.

BURGMEIER, J.W.; BOISEN, M.B., JR.; AND LARSEN, M.D. *Calculus with Applications.* New York, NY: McGraw-Hill, 1990.

FARLOW, STANLEY J. AND HAGGARD, GARY M. *Calculus and Its Applications.* New York, NY: McGraw-Hill, 1990.

HOFFMANN, LAURENCE D. AND BRADLEY, GERALD L. *Calculus for Business, Economics, and the Social and Life Sciences,* Fourth Edition. New York, NY: McGraw-Hill, 1986, 1989.

** STANCL, DONALD L. AND STANCL, MILDRED L. *Calculus for Management and the Life and Social Sciences,* Second Edition. Homewood, IL: Richard D. Irwin, 1988, 1990.

17.5 Finance

** BROVERMAN, SAMUEL A. *Mathematics of Investment and Finance.* Winsted, CT: ACTEX Publications, 1991.

BROWN, ROBERT L. AND ZIMA, P. *Mathematics of Finance.* New York, NY: McGraw-Hill, 1983.

BUTCHER, MARJORIE V. AND NESBITT, CECIL J. *Mathematics of Compound Interest.* Ann Arbor, MI: Ulrich's Bookstore, 1971.

* CISSELL, R.; CISSELL, H.; AND FLASPOHLER, D. *Mathematics of Finance,* Fifth Edition. Boston, MA: Houghton Mifflin, 1977.

CURTIS, A.B. AND COOPER, J. *Mathematics of Accounting,* Fourth Edition. Englewood Cliffs, NJ: Prentice Hall, 1961.

HART, W.L. *Mathematics of Investment,* Fifth Edition. Lexington, MA: D.C. Heath, 1975.

** KELLISON, STEPHEN G. *The Theory of Interest,* Second Edition. Homewood, IL: Richard D. Irwin, 1970, 1990.

McCUTCHEON, J.J. AND SCOTT, W.F. *An Introduction to the Mathematics of Finance.* London: Heinemann, 1986.

RINER, JOHN, *et al. Mathematics of Finance,* Fourth Edition. Englewood Cliffs, NJ: Prentice Hall, 1969.

17.6 Management

*** BOWEN, EARL K.; PRICHETT, GORDON D.; AND SABER, JOHN C. *Mathematics with Applications in Management and Economics,* Sixth Edition. Homewood, IL: Richard D. Irwin, 1972, 1987.

* COOKE, WILLIAM P. *Quantitative Methods for Management Decisions.* New York, NY: McGraw-Hill, 1985.

JOHNSON, R.H. AND WINN, P.R. *Quantitative Methods for Management.* Boston, MA: Houghton Mifflin, 1976.

* McDONALD, T.M. *Mathematical Models for Social and Management Scientists.* Boston, MA: Houghton Mifflin, 1974.

SPRINGER, C.H., *et al. Mathematics for Management Sciences,* 4 Vols. Homewood, IL: Richard D. Irwin, 1965–68.

17.7 Actuarial Mathematics

BEARD, R.E.; PENTAKAINEN, T.; AND PESONEN, E. *Risk Theory.* New York, NY: Chapman and Hall, 1984.

*** BOWERS, NEWTON L., JR., *et al. Actuarial Mathematics.* Itasca, IL: Society of Actuaries, 1984.

BUHLMAN, HANS. *Mathematical Methods in Risk Theory.* New York, NY: Springer-Verlag, 1970.

* CASUALTY ACTUARIAL SOCIETY. *Foundations of Casualty Actuarial Science.* Arlington, VA: Casualty Actuarial Society, 1990.

HOGG, ROBERT V. AND KLUGMAN, S. *Loss Distributions.* New York, NY: John Wiley, 1984.

Hustead, E.C. *100 Years of Mortality.* Schaumburg, IL: Society of Actuaries, 1989.

Jordan, C.W. *Life Contingencies,* Second Edition. Schaumburg, IL: Society of Actuaries, 1975.

Moorhead, E.J. *Our Yesterdays: The History of the Actuarial Profession in North America, 1805–1979.* Schaumburg, IL: Society of Actuaries, 1989.

Parmenter, Michael M. *Theory of Interest and Life Contingencies with Pension Applications: A Problem Solving Approach.* Winsted, CT: ACTEX Publications, 1988.

Trowbridge, Charles L. *Fundamental Concepts of Actuarial Science.* Schaumburg, IL: Actuarial Education and Research Fund, 1989.

18 Numerical Analysis

18.1 Introductory Texts

Atkinson, Kendall E. *Elementary Numerical Analysis.* New York, NY: John Wiley, 1978, 1985.

** Burden, Richard L. and Faires, J. Douglas. *Numerical Analysis,* Fourth Edition. Boston, MA: PWS-Kent, 1989.

Cheney, Elliot W. and Kincaid, David R. *Numerical Mathematics and Computing,* Second Edition. Pacific Grove, CA: Brooks/Cole, 1980, 1985.

Conte, Samuel D. and de Boor, Carl. *Elementary Numerical Analysis: An Algorithmic Approach,* Third Edition. New York, NY: McGraw-Hill, 1972, 1980.

* Davis, Philip F. and Rabinowitz, Philip. *Methods of Numerical Integration,* Second Edition. New York, NY: Academic Press, 1975, 1984.

Gerald, Curtis F. and Wheatley, Patrick O. *Applied Numerical Analysis,* Fourth Edition. Reading, MA: Addison-Wesley, 1978, 1989.

** Kincaid, David R. and Cheney, Elliot W. *Numerical Analysis: Mathematics of Scientific Computing.* Pacific Grove, CA: Brooks/Cole, 1991.

Mathews, John H. *Numerical Methods for Computer Science, Engineering, and Mathematics.* Englewood Cliffs, NJ: Prentice Hall, 1987.

Ralston, Anthony and Rabinowitz, Philip. *A First Course in Numerical Analysis,* Second Edition. New York, NY: McGraw-Hill, 1978.

18.2 Advanced Topics

Golub, Gene H., ed. *Studies in Numerical Analysis.* Washington, DC: Mathematical Association of America, 1984.

Greenspan, Donald and Casulli, Vincenzo. *Numerical Analysis for Applied Mathematics, Science, and Engineering.* Reading, MA: Addison-Wesley, 1988.

Sewell, Granville. *The Numerical Solution of Ordinary and Partial Differential Equations.* New York, NY: Academic Press, 1988.

18.3 Numerical Linear Algebra

* Golub, Gene H. and Van Loan, Charles F. *Matrix Computations,* Second Edition. Baltimore, MD: Johns Hopkins University Press, 1983, 1989.

Hill, David R. and Moler, Cleve B. *Experiments in Computational Matrix Algebra.* Cambridge, MA: Random House, 1987.

Rice, John R. *Matrix Computations and Mathematical Software.* New York, NY: McGraw-Hill, 1981.

Wilkinson, James H. *The Algebraic Eigenvalue Problem.* New York, NY: Oxford University Press, 1965, 1988.

18.4 Approximation Theory

CHENEY, ELLIOT W. *Introduction to Approximation Theory*, Second Edition. New York, NY: Chelsea, 1966, 1982.

DAVIS, PHILIP J. *Interpolation and Approximation*. Mineola, NY: Dover, 1975.

18.5 Computer Methods

FRÖBERG, CARL-ERIK. *Numerical Mathematics: Theory and Computer Applications*. Redwood City, CA: Benjamin Cummings, 1985.

GRANDINE, THOMAS A. *The Numerical Methods Programming Projects Book*. New York, NY: Oxford University Press, 1990.

MOHAMED, J.L. AND WALSH, J.E., EDS. *Numerical Algorithms*. New York, NY: Clarendon Press, 1986.

PRESS, WILLIAM H., *et al. Numerical Recipes: The Art of Scientific Computing*. New York, NY: Cambridge University Press, 1986.

19 Modeling and Operations Research

19.1 General

* DANTZIG, GEORGE B. AND EAVES, B.C., EDS. *Studies in Optimization*. Washington, DC: Mathematical Association of America, 1974.

FRENCH, SIMON. *Readings in Decision Analysis*. New York, NY: Chapman and Hall, 1989.

* GASS, SAUL I. *Decision Making, Models, and Algorithms: A First Course*. New York, NY: John Wiley, 1985.

*** HILLIER, FREDERICK S. AND LIEBERMAN, GERALD J. *Introduction to Operations Research*, Fifth Edition. Oakland, CA: Holden-Day, 1974; New York, NY: McGraw-Hill, 1990.

** WAGNER, HARVEY M. *Principles of Operations Research with Applications to Managerial Decisions*, Second Edition. Englewood Cliffs, NJ: Prentice Hall, 1969, 1975.

WINSTON, WAYNE L. *Operations Research: Applications and Algorithms*, Second Edition. Boston, MA: Duxbury Press, 1987; Boston, MA: PWS-Kent, 1991.

19.2 Mathematical Modeling

ANDREWS, J.G. AND McLONE, R.R., EDS. *Mathematical Modelling*. Woburn, MA: Butterworth, 1976.

BELTRAMI, EDWARD J. *Mathematics for Dynamic Modeling*. New York, NY: Academic Press, 1987.

BOYCE, WILLIAM E., ED. *Case Studies in Mathematical Modeling*. Brooklyn, NY: Pitman, 1981.

** BRAUN, MARTIN; COLEMAN, COURTNEY S.; AND DREW, DONALD A., EDS. *Differential Equation Models*. Modules in Applied Mathematics, Vol. 1. New York, NY: Springer-Verlag, 1983.

CROSS, MARK AND MOSCARDINI, A.O. *Learning the Art of Mathematical Modelling*. New York, NY: Halsted Press, 1985.

* GIORDANO, FRANK R. AND WEIR, MAURICE D. *A First Course in Mathematical Modeling*. Pacific Grove, CA: Brooks/Cole, 1985.

* HABERMAN, RICHARD. *Mathematical Models, Mechanical Vibrations, Population Dynamics, and Traffic Flow: An Introduction to Applied Mathematics*. Englewood Cliffs, NJ: Prentice Hall, 1977.

* KLAMKIN, MURRAY S. *Mathematical Modelling: Classroom Notes in Applied Mathematics*. Philadelphia, PA: Society for Industrial and Applied Mathematics, 1987.

* LUCAS, WILLIAM F.; ROBERTS, FRED S.; AND THRALL, ROBERT M., EDS. *Discrete and System Models*. Modules in Applied Mathematics, Vol. 3. New York, NY: Springer-Verlag, 1983.

MELZAK, Z.A. *Mathematical Ideas, Modeling, and Applications*. New York, NY: John Wiley, 1976.

MEYER, WALTER J. *Concepts of Mathematical Modeling*. New York, NY: McGraw-Hill, 1984.

* POSTON, TIM AND STEWART, IAN. *Catastrophe Theory and its Applications*. Brooklyn, NY: Pitman, 1978.

* ROBERTS, FRED S. *Discrete Mathematical Models with Applications to Social, Biological, and Environmental Problems*. Englewood Cliffs, NJ: Prentice Hall, 1976.

SAATY, THOMAS L. AND ALEXANDER, JOYCE M. *Thinking With Models: Mathematical Models in the Physical, Biological, and Social Sciences*. Elmsford, NY: Pergamon Press, 1981.

STARFIELD, ANTHONY M.; SMITH, KARL A.; AND BLELOCH, ANDREW L. *How to Model It: Problem Solving for the Computer Age*. New York, NY: McGraw-Hill, 1990.

WAN, FREDERIC Y.M. *Mathematical Models and Their Analysis*. New York, NY: Harper and Row, 1989.

WILLIAMS, H.P. *Model Building in Mathematical Programming*, Second Edition. New York, NY: John Wiley, 1978, 1985.

** WOODCOCK, ALEXANDER AND DAVIS, MONTE. *Catastrophe Theory*. New York, NY: E.P. Dutton, 1978.

19.3 Game Theory

AUMANN, ROBERT J. AND HART, SERGIU. *Handbook of Game Theory with Applications to Economics*, Amsterdam: North-Holland, 1991.

BRAMS, STEVEN J. AND KILGOUR, D. MARC. *Game Theory and National Security*. Cambridge, MA: Basil Blackwell, 1988.

DAVIS, MORTON D. *Game Theory: A Nontechnical Introduction*. New York, NY: Basic Books, 1970.

LUCAS, WILLIAM F., ED. *Game Theory and its Applications*. Providence, RI: American Mathematical Society, 1981.

** LUCE, ROBERT DUNCAN AND RAIFFA, HOWARD. *Games and Decisions*. New York, NY: John Wiley, 1957.

MCDONALD, JOHN. *The Game of Business*. New York, NY: Doubleday, 1975.

RUCKLE, W.H. *Geometric Games and Their Applications*. Brooklyn, NY: Pitman, 1983.

* WILLIAMS, JOHN D. *The Compleat Strategyst: Being a Primer on the Theory of Games of Strategy*. New York, NY: McGraw-Hill, 1954; Mineola, NY: Dover, 1986.

19.4 Linear Programming

** CHVÁTAL, VASEK. *Linear Programming*. New York, NY: W.H. Freeman, 1983.

* DANTZIG, GEORGE B. *Linear Programming and Extensions*. Princeton, NJ: Princeton University Press, 1963.

GASS, SAUL I. *Linear Programming: Methods and Applications*, Fifth Edition. New York, NY: McGraw-Hill, 1969, 1985.

KOLMAN, BERNARD AND BECK, ROBERT E. *Elementary Linear Programming with Applications*, New York, NY: Academic Press, 1980.

19.5 Special Topics

BRATLEY, PAUL; FOX, BENNETT L.; AND SCHRAGE, LINUS E. *A Guide to Simulation*. New York, NY: Springer-Verlag, 1983.

FISHMAN, G.S. *Principles of Discrete Event Simulation*. New York, NY: John Wiley, 1978.

GAZIS, DENOS C., ED. *Traffic Science*. New York, NY: John Wiley, 1974.

** GROSS, DONALD AND HARRIS, CARL M. *Fundamentals of Queueing Theory*, Second Edition. New York, NY: John Wiley, 1974, 1985.

HEYMAN, D.P. AND SOBEL, M.J. *Handbook in Operations Research and Management Science*. Amsterdam: North-Holland, 1989.

* LAWLER, EUGENE L., et al., EDS. *The Traveling Salesman Problem: A Guided Tour of Combinatorial Optimization*. New York, NY: John Wiley, 1985.

* NEMHAUSER, GEORGE L. AND WOLSEY, LAURENCE A. *Integer and Combinatorial Optimization.* New York, NY: John Wiley, 1988.

RIPLEY, BRIAN D. *Stochastic Simulation.* New York, NY: John Wiley, 1987.

RUBINSTEIN, REUVEN Y. *Simulation and the Monte Carlo Method.* New York, NY: John Wiley, 1981.

SAATY, THOMAS L. AND BRAM, JOSEPH. *Nonlinear Mathematics.* Mineola, NY: Dover, 1981.

SIMMONS, DONALD M. *Nonlinear Programming for Operations Research.* Englewood Cliffs, NJ: Prentice Hall, 1975.

20 Probability

20.1 General

CACOULLOS, T. *Exercises in Probability.* New York, NY: Springer-Verlag, 1989.

* DAVID, F.N. *Games, Gods, and Gambling.* New York, NY: Hafner Press, 1962.

GANI, J., ED. *The Craft of Probabilistic Modelling: A Collection of Personal Accounts.* New York, NY: Springer-Verlag, 1986.

** GNANADESIKAN, MRUDULLA; SCHEAFFER, RICHARD L.; AND SWIFT, JIM. *The Art and Techniques of Simulation.* Palo Alto, CA: Dale Seymour, 1987.

HUFF, DARRELL AND GEIS, I. *How to Take a Chance.* New York, NY: W.W. Norton, 1959.

KAHNEMAN, DANIEL; SLOVIC, PAUL; AND TVERSKY, AMOS, EDS. *Judgment Under Uncertainty: Heuristics and Biases.* New York, NY: Cambridge University Press, 1982.

* MOSTELLER, FREDERICK. *Fifty Challenging Problems in Probability with Solutions.* Mineola, NY: Dover, 1987.

** NEWMAN, CLAIRE M.; OBREMSKI, THOMAS E.; AND SCHEAFFER, RICHARD L. *Exploring Probability.* Palo Alto, CA: Dale Seymour, 1987.

*** PACKEL, EDWARD W. *The Mathematics of Games and Gambling.* Washington, DC: Mathematical Association of America, 1981.

** WEAVER, WARREN. *Lady Luck: The Theory of Probability.* Mineola, NY: Dover, 1982.

20.2 Elementary

** CHUNG, KAI LAI. *Elementary Probability Theory with Stochastic Processes,* Third Edition. New York, NY: Springer-Verlag, 1974, 1979.

GNEDENKO, BORIS V. AND KHINCHIN, A. YA. *An Elementary Introduction to the Theory of Probability.* Mineola, NY: Dover, 1962.

HODGES, JOSEPH L. AND LEHMANN, E.L. *Elements of Finite Probability,* Second Edition. San Francisco, CA: Holden-Day, 1970.

MOSTELLER, FREDERICK, *et al. Probability with Statistical Applications,* Second Edition. Reading, MA: Addison-Wesley, 1970.

ROSS, SHELDON M. *Introduction to Probability Models,* Third Edition. New York, NY: Academic Press, 1972, 1985.

** SCHEAFFER, RICHARD L. *Introduction to Probability and Its Applications.* Boston, MA: PWS-Kent, 1990.

** SNELL, J. LAURIE. *Introduction to Probability.* Cambridge, MA: Random House, 1988.

20.3 Advanced

DURRETT, RICHARD. *Probability: Theory and Examples.* Belmont, CA: Wadsworth, 1991.

** FELLER, WILLIAM. *An Introduction to Probability Theory and Its Applications,* 2 Vols., Second Edition. New York, NY: John Wiley, 1968, 1971.

GNEDENKO, BORIS V. *The Theory of Probability and the Elements of Statistics*, Fifth Edition. Moscow: MIR, 1976; New York, NY: Chelsea, 1967, 1989.

* KAC, MARK. *Statistical Independence in Probability, Analysis, and Number Theory*. Washington, DC: Mathematical Association of America, 1959.

ROTHSCHILD, V. AND LOGOTHETIS, N. *Probability Distributions*. New York, NY: John Wiley, 1986.

20.4 Stochastic Processes

DOYLE, PETER G. AND SNELL, J. LAURIE. *Random Walks and Electric Networks*. Washington, DC: Mathematical Association of America, 1984.

DUBINS, LESTER E. AND SAVAGE, LEONARD J. *Inequalities for Stochastic Processes (How to Gamble If You Must)*. New York, NY: McGraw-Hill, 1965; Mineola, NY: Dover, 1976.

KEMENY, JOHN G. AND SNELL, J. LAURIE. *Finite Markov Chains*. New York, NY: Springer-Verlag, 1976.

SOBOL, I.M. *The Monte Carlo Method*. Chicago, IL: University of Chicago Press, 1974; Moscow: MIR, 1975.

TAYLOR, HOWARD M. AND KARLIN, SAMUEL. *An Introduction to Stochastic Modeling*. New York, NY: Academic Press, 1984.

20.5 Foundations

GOOD, I.J. *Good Thinking: The Foundations of Probability and Its Applications*. Minneapolis, MN: University of Minnesota Press, 1983.

* KOLMOGOROV, ANDREI N. *Foundations of the Theory of Probability*, Second Edition. New York, NY: Chelsea, 1950, 1956.

** VON MISES, RICHARD. *Probability, Statistics, and Truth*, Second Revised English Edition. New York, NY: Macmillan, 1957; Mineola, NY: Dover, 1981.

20.6 Special Topics

BILLINGSLEY, PATRICK. *Probability and Measure*, Second Edition. New York, NY: John Wiley, 1979, 1986.

ROMANO, JOSEPH P. AND SIEGEL, ANDREW F. *Counterexamples in Probability and Statistics*. Belmont, CA: Wadsworth, 1986.

SZÉKELY, GÁBOR J. *Paradoxes in Probability Theory and Mathematical Statistics*. Norwell, MA: D. Reidel, 1986.

* YAGLOM, A.M. AND YAGLOM, I.M. *Probability and Information*. Norwell, MA: D. Reidel, 1983.

21 Statistics

21.1 General

BROOK, RICHARD J., et al., EDS. *The Fascination of Statistics*. New York, NY: Marcel Dekker, 1986.

DEGROOT, MORRIS H.; FIENBERG, STEPHEN E.; AND KADANE, JOSEPH B., EDS. *Statistics and the Law*. New York, NY: John Wiley, 1986.

* DEMING, W. EDWARDS. *Out of The Crisis*. Cambridge, MA: MIT Press, 1986.

HOGG, ROBERT V., ED. *Studies in Statistics*. Washington, DC: Mathematical Association of America, 1978.

HOLLANDER, MYLES AND PROSCHAN, FRANK. *The Statistical Exorcist: Dispelling Statistics Anxiety*. New York, NY: Marcel Dekker, 1984.

HUFF, DARRELL AND GEIS, I. *How to Lie with Statistics*. New York, NY: W.W. Norton, 1954.

* JAFFE, A.J. AND SPIRER, HERBERT F. *Misused Statistics: Straight Talk for Twisted Numbers.* New York, NY: Marcel Dekker, 1987.

** LANDWEHR, JAMES M. AND WATKINS, ANN E. *Exploring Data.* Palo Alto, CA: Dale Seymour, 1986.

** LANDWEHR, JAMES M.; SWIFT, JIM; AND WATKINS, ANN E. *Exploring Surveys and Information From Samples.* Palo Alto, CA: Dale Seymour, 1987.

*** TANUR, JUDITH M. AND MOSTELLER, FREDERICK, EDS. *Statistics: A Guide to the Unknown,* Third Edition. San Francisco, CA: Holden-Day, 1972; Belmont, CA: Wadsworth, 1989.

** TUFTE, EDWARD R. *Envisioning Information.* Cheshire, CT: Graphics Press, 1990.

*** TUFTE, EDWARD R. *The Visual Display of Quantitative Information.* Cheshire, CT: Graphics Press, 1983.

21.2 Introductory Texts

DEVORE, JAY L. AND PECK, ROXY. *Statistics: The Exploration and Analysis of Data.* St. Paul, MN: West, 1986.

** FREEDMAN, DAVID, *et al. Statistics,* Second Edition. New York, NY: W.W. Norton, 1978, 1991.

** KOOPMANS, LAMBERT H. *Introduction to Contemporary Statistical Methods,* Second Edition. Boston, MA: PWS-Kent, 1987.

McCLAVE, JAMES T. AND DIETRICH, FRANK H. *Statistics,* Fifth Edition. San Francisco, CA: Dellen, 1982, 1991.

* MOORE, DAVID S. AND McCABE, GEORGE P. *Introduction to the Practice of Statistics.* New York, NY: W.H. Freeman, 1989.

*** MOORE, DAVID S. *Statistics: Concepts and Controversies,* Third Edition. New York, NY: W.H. Freeman, 1979, 1991.

NOETHER, GOTTFRIED. *Introduction to Statistics: A Fresh Approach.* Boston, MA: Houghton Mifflin, 1971; New York, NY: Springer-Verlag, 1991.

21.3 Elementary

CHATFIELD, CHRISTOPHER. *Problem Solving: A Statistician's Guide.* New York, NY: Chapman and Hall, 1988.

* LARSEN, RICHARD J. AND STROUP, DONNA F. *Statistics in the Real World: A Book of Examples.* New York, NY: Macmillan, 1976.

* MOSES, LINCOLN E. *Think and Explain with Statistics.* Reading, MA: Addison-Wesley, 1986.

YOUDEN, W.J. *Experimentation and Measurement.* Washington, DC: National Bureau of Standards, 1984.

* YOUDEN, W.J. *Risk, Choice, and Prediction: An Introduction to Experimentation.* Boston, MA: Duxbury Press, 1974.

21.4 Intermediate

* BOX, GEORGE E.P.; HUNTER, WILLIAM G.; AND HUNTER, J. STUART. *Statistics for Experimenters: An Introduction to Design, Data Analysis, and Model Building.* New York, NY: John Wiley, 1978.

DEVORE, JAY L. *Probability and Statistics for Engineering and the Sciences,* Third Edition. Pacific Grove, CA: Brooks/Cole, 1982, 1991.

HOGG, ROBERT V. AND CRAIG, ALLEN T. *Introduction to Mathematical Statistics,* Fourth Edition. New York, NY: Macmillan, 1958, 1978.

HOGG, ROBERT V. AND LEDOLTER, JOHANNES. *Engineering Statistics.* New York, NY: Macmillan, 1987.

* HOGG, ROBERT V. AND TANIS, ELLIOT A. *Probability and Statistical Inference,* Third Edition. New York, NY: Macmillan, 1977, 1988.

MENDENHALL, WILLIAM; WACKERLY, DENNIS D.; AND SCHEAFFER, RICHARD L. *Mathematical Statistics with Applications,* Fourth Edition. Boston, MA: PWS-Kent, 1990.

RAO, C. RADHKIRSHNA. *Linear Statistical Inference and Its Applications,* Second Edition. New York, NY: John Wiley, 1973.

** SNEDECOR, GEORGE W. AND COCHRAN, WILLIAM G. *Statistical Methods,* Seventh Edition. Ames, IA: Iowa State University Press, 1967, 1980.

21.5 Data Analysis

CHAMBERS, JOHN M., *et al. Graphical Methods for Data Analysis.* Belmont, CA: Wadsworth, 1983.

* CLEVELAND, WILLIAM S. *The Elements of Graphing Data,* Second Edition. Belmont, CA: Wadsworth, 1985, 1991.

EFRON, BRADLEY. *The Jackknife, the Bootstrap, and Other Resampling Plans.* Philadelphia, PA: Society for Industrial and Applied Mathematics, 1982.

* HOAGLIN, DAVID C.; MOSTELLER, FREDERICK; AND TUKEY, JOHN W., EDS. *Understanding Robust and Exploratory Data Analysis.* New York, NY: John Wiley, 1983.

MOSTELLER, FREDERICK; FIENBERG, STEPHEN E.; AND ROURKE, ROBERT E.K. *Beginning Statistics with Data Analysis.* Reading, MA: Addison-Wesley, 1983.

VELLEMAN, PAUL F. AND HOAGLIN, DAVID C. *Applications, Basics, and Computing of Exploratory Data Analysis.* Boston, MA: Duxbury Press, 1981.

21.6 Linear Models and Regression Analysis

DRAPER, NORMAN R. AND SMITH, H. *Applied Regression Analysis,* Second Edition. New York, NY: John Wiley, 1981.

** MOSTELLER, FREDERICK AND TUKEY, JOHN W. *Data Analysis and Regression: A Second Course in Statistics.* Reading, MA: Addison-Wesley, 1977.

WEISBERG, SANFORD. *Applied Linear Regression,* Second Edition. New York, NY: John Wiley, 1980, 1985.

21.7 Sampling and Survey Design

COCHRAN, WILLIAM G. *Sampling Techniques,* Third Edition. New York, NY: John Wiley, 1977.

DEMING, W. EDWARDS. *Some Theory of Sampling.* Mineola, NY: Dover, 1966.

* SCHEAFFER, RICHARD L.; MENDENHALL, WILLIAM; AND OTT, LYMAN. *Elementary Survey Sampling.* Belmont, CA: Wadsworth, 1971; Boston, MA: PWS-Kent, 1990.

* WILLIAMS, BILL. *A Sampler on Sampling.* New York, NY: John Wiley, 1978.

21.8 Special Topics

FISHER, RONALD A. *Statistical Methods, Experimental Design, and Scientific Inference,* Combined Edition. New York, NY: Hafner Press, 1959; New York, NY: Oxford University Press, 1990.

IVERSON, GUDMUND R. *Bayesian Statistical Inference.* Beverly Hills, CA: Sage, 1984.

JOHNSON, RICHARD A. AND WICHERN, DEAN W. *Applied Multivariate Statistical Analysis,* Second Edition. Englewood Cliffs, NJ: Prentice Hall, 1982, 1988.

LEHMANN, E.L. AND D'ABRERA, H.J.M. *Nonparametrics: Statistical Methods Based on Ranks.* San Francisco, CA: Holden-Day, 1975.

22 Computer Science

22.1 Computer Literacy

ARGANBRIGHT, DEAN E. *Mathematical Applications of Electronic Spreadsheets.* New York, NY: McGraw-Hill, 1985.

* BIERMAN, ALAN. *Great Ideas in Computer Science.* Cambridge, MA: MIT Press, 1990.

BRUCE, J.W.; GIBLIN, P.J.; AND RIPPON, P.J. *Microcomputers and Mathematics.* New York, NY: Cambridge University Press, 1990.

* DECKER, RICK AND HIRSHFIELD, STUART. *The Analytical Engine.* Belmont, CA: Wadsworth, 1990.

*** DEWDNEY, A.K. *The Armchair Universe: An Exploration of Computer Worlds.* New York, NY: W.H. Freeman, 1988.

*** DEWDNEY, A.K. *The Turing Omnibus: 61 Excursions in Computer Science.* Rockville, MD: Computer Science Press, 1989.

GRAY, THEODORE W. AND GLYNN, JERRY. *Exploring Mathematics with Mathematica: Dialogs Concerning Computers and Mathematics.* Reading, MA: Addison-Wesley, 1991.

* HAREL, DAVID. *Algorithmics: The Spirit of Computing.* Reading, MA: Addison-Wesley, 1987.

KIDDER, TRACY. *The Soul of a New Machine.* Waltham, MA: Little, Brown, 1981.

MOREAU, R. *The Computer Comes of Age: The People, the Hardware, and the Software.* Cambridge, MA: MIT Press, 1984.

* VON NEUMANN, JOHN. *The Computer and the Brain,* New Haven, CT: Yale University Press, 1979.

* WEISS, ERIC A., ED. *A Computer Science Reader: Selections from Abacus.* New York, NY: Springer-Verlag, 1988.

22.2 Computers and Society

* BOLTER, J. DAVID. *Turing's Man: Western Culture in the Computer Age.* Chapel Hill, NC: University of North Carolina Press, 1984.

KEMENY, JOHN G. *Man and the Computer.* New York, NY: Charles Scribner's, 1972.

* ROSZAK, THEODORE. *The Cult of Information: The Folklore of Computers and the True Art of Thinking.* Cambridge, MA: Pantheon Books, 1986.

*** STOLL, CLIFFORD. *The Cuckoo's Egg: Tracking a Spy Through the Maze of Computer Espionage.* New York, NY: Doubleday, 1989.

** WEIZENBAUM, JOSEPH. *Computer Power and Human Reason: From Judgment to Calculation.* New York, NY: W.H. Freeman, 1976.

22.3 Introductory

** ABELSON, HAROLD; SUSSMAN, GERALD J.; AND SUSSMAN, JULIE. *Structure and Interpretation of Computer Programs.* Cambridge, MA: MIT Press, 1985.

McGETTRICK, ANDREW D. AND SMITH, PETER D. *Graded Problems in Computer Science.* Reading, MA: Addison-Wesley, 1983.

POLLACK, SEYMOUR V., ED. *Studies in Computer Science.* Washington, DC: Mathematical Association of America, 1982.

* TUCKER, ALLEN B., *et al. Fundamentals of Computing I: Logic, Problem-Solving, Programs, and Computers.* New York, NY: McGraw-Hill, 1991.

WULF, WILLIAM A., *et al. Fundamental Structures of Computer Science.* Reading, MA: Addison-Wesley, 1981.

22.4 Data Structures

*** AHO, ALFRED V.; HOPCROFT, JOHN E.; AND ULLMAN, JEFFREY D. *Data Structures and Algorithms.* Reading, MA: Addison-Wesley, 1983.

HOROWITZ, ELLIS AND SAHNI, SARTAJ. *Fundamentals of Data Structures in Pascal,* Third Edition. Rockville, MD: Computer Science Press, 1976, 1990.

KORSH, JAMES F. AND GARRETT, LEONARD J. *Data Structures, Algorithms, and Program Style Using C.* Boston, MA: PWS-Kent, 1986, 1988.

* KRUSE, ROBERT L. *Data Structures and Program Design,* Second Edition. Englewood Cliffs, NJ: Prentice Hall, 1984, 1987.

MEHLHORN, KURT. *Data Structures and Algorithms,* 3 Vols. New York, NY: Springer-Verlag, 1984.

MILLER, NANCY E. *File Structures Using Pascal.* Redwood City, CA: Benjamin Cummings, 1987.

STUBBS, DAVID F. AND WEBRE, NEIL W. *Data Structures,* Second Edition. Pacific Grove, CA: Brooks/Cole, 1989.

* WIRTH, NIKLAUS. *Algorithms and Data Structures.* (Former title: *Algorithms + Data Structures = Programs.*) Englewood Cliffs, NJ: Prentice Hall, 1976, 1986.

22.5 Database Systems

* DATE, C.J. *An Introduction to Database Systems,* Fourth Edition. Reading, MA: Addison-Wesley, 1981, 1986.

KORTH, HENRY F. AND SILBERSCHATZ, ABRAHAM. *Database System Concepts.* New York, NY: McGraw-Hill, 1986.

ULLMAN, JEFFREY D. *Principals of Database and Knowledge-based Systems,* 2 Vols. Rockville, MD: Computer Science Press, 1988.

22.6 Programming

** BENTLEY, JON. *More Programming Pearls.* Reading, MA: Addison-Wesley, 1988.

** BENTLEY, JON. *Programming Pearls.* Reading, MA: Addison-Wesley, 1986.

BRAWER, STEVEN. *Introduction to Parallel Programming.* New York, NY: Academic Press, 1989.

COX, BRAD J. *Object-Oriented Programming: An Evolutionary Approach.* Reading, MA: Addison-Wesley, 1986.

DAHL, O.J.; DIJKSTRA, EDSGER W.; AND HOARE, C.A.R. *Structured Programming.* New York, NY: Academic Press, 1972.

DIJKSTRA, EDSGER W. *A Discipline of Programming.* Englewood Cliffs, NJ: Prentice Hall, 1976.

** HOROWITZ, ELLIS, ED. *Programming Languages: A Grand Tour,* Third Edition. Rockville, MD: Computer Science Press, 1983, 1987.

*** KERNIGHAN, BRIAN W. AND PLAUGER, P.J. *The Elements of Programming Style,* Second Edition. New York, NY: McGraw-Hill, 1974, 1978.

MACLENNAN, BRUCE J. *Principles of Programming Languages: Design, Evaluation, and Implementation,* Second Edition. New York, NY: Holt, Rinehart and Winston, 1983, 1986.

* MEYER, BERTRAND. *Introduction to the Theory of Programming Languages.* Englewood Cliffs, NJ: Prentice Hall, 1990.

* WEXELBLAT, RICHARD L., ED. *History of Programming Languages.* New York, NY: Academic Press, 1981.

22.7 Programming Languages

* CLOCKSIN, W.F. AND MELLISH, C.S. *Programming in Prolog,* Third Revised Edition. New York, NY: Springer-Verlag, 1981, 1987.

* COOPER, D. *Standard Pascal: User Reference Manual.* New York, NY: W.W. Norton, 1983.

GOLDBERG, ADELE AND ROBSON, DAVID. *Smalltalk-80: The Language.* Reading, MA: Addison-Wesley, 1983, 1989.

* KERNIGHAN, BRIAN W. AND RITCHIE, DENNIS M. *The C Programming Language,* Second Edition. Englewood Cliffs, NJ: Prentice Hall, 1988.

KOFFMAN, ELLIOT B. *Pascal: Problem Solving and Program Design,* Third Edition. Reading, MA: Addison-Wesley, 1989.

POLIVKA, RAYMOND AND PAKIN, SANDRA. *APL: The Language and Its Usage.* Englewood Cliffs, NJ: Prentice Hall, 1975.

SHUMATE, K. *Understanding Ada with Abstract Data Types.* New York, NY: John Wiley, 1989.

* WINSTON, PATRICK H.; KLAUS, BERTHOLD; AND HORN, PAUL. *LISP,* Third Edition. Reading, MA: Addison-Wesley, 1981, 1989.

* WIRTH, NIKLAUS. *Programming in Modula-2,* Fourth Edition. New York, NY: Springer-Verlag, 1982, 1988.

22.8 Algorithms

** AHO, ALFRED V.; HOPCROFT, JOHN E.; AND ULLMAN, JEFFREY D. *The Design and Analysis of Computer Algorithms.* Reading, MA: Addison-Wesley, 1974.

BAASE, SARA. *Computer Algorithms: Introduction to Design and Analysis,* Second Edition. Reading, MA: Addison-Wesley, 1978, 1988.

BERLIOUX, PIERRE AND BIZARD, PHILIPPE. *Algorithms: The Construction, Proof, and Analysis of Programs.* New York, NY: John Wiley, 1986.

BRASSARD, GILLES AND BRATLEY, PAUL. *Algorithmics: Theory and Practice.* Englewood Cliffs, NJ: Prentice Hall, 1988.

DAVENPORT, J.H.; SIRET, Y.; AND TOURNIER, E. *Computer Algebra: Systems and Algorithms for Algebraic Computation.* New York, NY: Academic Press, 1988.

*** KNUTH, DONALD E. *The Art of Computer Programming,* 3 Vols., Second Edition. Reading, MA: Addison-Wesley, 1969–81.

* MANBER, UDI. *Introduction to Algorithms: A Creative Approach.* Reading, MA: Addison-Wesley, 1989.

* REINGOLD, EDWARD M.; NIEVERGELT, JURG; AND DEO, NARSINGH. *Combinatorial Algorithms: Theory and Practice.* Englewood Cliffs, NJ: Prentice Hall, 1977.

* SEDGEWICK, ROBERT. *Algorithms in C.* Reading, MA: Addison-Wesley, 1990.

WILF, HERBERT S. *Algorithms and Complexity.* Englewood Cliffs, NJ: Prentice Hall, 1986.

22.9 Theory of Computation

DAVIS, MARTIN D. AND WEYUKER, ELAINE J. *Computability, Complexity, and Languages: Fundamentals of Theoretical Computer Science.* New York, NY: Academic Press, 1983.

* GAREY, MICHAEL R. AND JOHNSON, DAVID S. *Computers and Intractability: A Guide to the Theory of NP-Completeness.* New York, NY: W.H. Freeman, 1979.

WINOGRAD, SHMUEL. *Arithmetic Complexity of Computations.* Philadelphia, PA: Society for Industrial and Applied Mathematics, 1980.

22.10 Software Systems

* DEITEL, HARVEY M. *Operating Systems,* Second Edition. Reading, MA: Addison-Wesley, 1984, 1990.

KERNIGHAN, BRIAN W. AND PIKE, ROB. *The UNIX Programming Environment.* Englewood Cliffs, NJ: Prentice Hall, 1984.

22.11 Artificial Intelligence

ARBIB, MICHAEL A. *Brains, Machines, and Mathematics,* Second Edition. New York, NY: McGraw-Hill, 1964; New York, NY: Springer-Verlag, 1987.

* BARR, AVRON; COHEN, PAUL R.; AND FEIGENBAUM, EDWARD A., EDS. *The Handbook of Artificial Intelligence*, 4 Vols. Los Altos, CA: William Kaufmann, 1981–82; Reading, MA: Addison-Wesley, 1989.

LEVY, DAVID N.L., ED. *Computer Games I.* New York, NY: Springer-Verlag, 1988.

MINSKY, MARVIN AND PAPERT, SEYMOUR. *Perceptrons: An Introduction to Computational Geometry,* Expanded Edition. Cambridge, MA: MIT Press, 1988.

* WINSTON, PATRICK H. AND BROWN, RICHARD H., EDS. *Artificial Intelligence: An MIT Perspective,* 2 Vols., Second Edition. Cambridge, MA: MIT Press, 1979, 1984.

** WINSTON, PATRICK H. *Artificial Intelligence.* Reading, MA: Addison-Wesley, 1977.

22.12 Software Engineering

* GRIES, DAVID. *The Science of Programming.* New York, NY: Springer-Verlag, 1981.

PRESSMAN, R. *Software Engineering: A Practitioner's Approach.* New York, NY: McGraw-Hill, 1987.

SOMMERVILLE, IAN. *Software Engineering,* Second Edition. Reading, MA: Addison-Wesley, 1985.

22.13 Compilers and Translators

** AHO, ALFRED V.; SETHI, RAVI; AND ULLMAN, JEFFREY D. *Compilers: Principles, Techniques, and Tools.* (Former title: *Principles of Compiler Design.*) Reading, MA: Addison-Wesley, 1978, 1986.

FISCHER, CHARLES N. AND LEBLANC, RICHARD J., JR. *Crafting a Compiler.* Redwood City, CA: Benjamin Cummings, 1988.

TREMBLAY, JEAN-PAUL. *Theory and Practice of Compiler Writing.* New York, NY: McGraw-Hill, 1985.

WAITE, WILLIAM M. AND GOOS, GERHARD. *Compiler Construction.* New York, NY: Springer-Verlag, 1984.

22.14 Computer Graphics

FIUME, EUGENE L. *The Mathematical Structure of Raster Graphics.* New York, NY: Academic Press, 1989.

** FOLEY, JAMES D., et al. *Computer Graphics: Principles and Practice.* Reading, MA: Addison-Wesley, 1990.

GLASSNER, ANDREW, ED. *Graphics Gems.* New York, NY: Academic Press, 1990.

GLASSNER, ANDREW. *An Introduction to Ray Tracing.* New York, NY: Academic Press, 1989.

* HEARN, DONALD AND BAKER, PAULINE. *Computer Graphics.* Englewood Cliffs, NJ: Prentice Hall, 1986.

* WATT, ALAN. *Fundamentals of Three Dimensional Computer Graphics.* Reading, MA: Addison-Wesley, 1990.

22.15 Special Topics

** HOPCROFT, JOHN E. AND ULLMAN, JEFFREY D. *Introduction to Automata Theory, Languages, and Computation.* Reading, MA: Addison-Wesley, 1979.

KNUTH, DONALD E. *The TEX Book.* Reading, MA: Addison-Wesley, 1986.

SPIVAK, MICHAEL D. *The Joy of TEX: A Gourmet Guide to Typesetting with the AMS-TEX Macro Package,* Second Edition. Providence, RI: American Mathematical Society, 1986, 1990.

* TANENBAUM, ANDREW S. *Structured Computer Organization,* Third Edition. Englewood Cliffs, NJ: Prentice Hall, 1976, 1989.

23 Applications to Life Sciences

23.1 General

BERG, H.C. *Random Walks in Biology*. Princeton, NJ: Princeton University Press, 1983.

* CASTI, JOHN L. *Alternate Realities: Mathematical Models of Nature and Man*. New York, NY: John Wiley, 1989.

CULLEN, MICHAEL R. *Mathematics for the Biosciences*. Boston, MA: Prindle, Weber and Schmidt, 1983.

* EDELSTEIN-KESHET, LEAH. *Mathematical Models in Biology*. Cambridge, MA: Random House, 1988.

* LEVIN, SIMON A., ED. *Studies in Mathematical Biology*, 2 Vols. Washington, DC: Mathematical Association of America, 1978.

LOTKA, A.J. *Elements of Mathematical Biology*. Mineola, NY: Dover, 1956.

** MARCUS-ROBERTS, HELEN AND THOMPSON, MAYNARD, EDS. *Life Science Models*. Modules in Applied Mathematics, Vol. 4. New York, NY: Springer-Verlag, 1983.

* MURRAY, J.D. *Mathematical Biology*. New York, NY: Springer-Verlag, 1989.

*** TANUR, JUDITH M., *et al.*, EDS. *Statistics: A Guide to the Study of the Biological and Health Sciences*. San Francisco, CA: Holden-Day, 1977.

23.2 Ecology

GAUSE, G.F. *The Struggle for Existence*. Baltimore, MD: Williams and Wilkins, 1934; Mineola, NY: Dover, 1971.

* HALLAM, THOMAS G. AND LEVIN, SIMON A., EDS. *Mathematical Ecology: An Introduction*. New York, NY: Springer-Verlag, 1986.

KINGSLAND, SHARON E. *Modeling Nature: Episodes in the History of Population Ecology*. Chicago, IL: University of Chicago Press, 1985.

MANGEL, MARC AND CLARK, COLIN W. *Dynamic Modeling in Behavioral Ecology*. Princeton, NJ: Princeton University Press, 1988.

OSTER, GEORGE F. AND WILSON, EDWARD O. *Caste and Ecology in the Social Insects*. Princeton, NJ: Princeton University Press, 1978.

PRUSINKIEWICZ, PRZEMYSLAW AND HANAN, JAMES. *Lindenmayer Systems, Fractals, and Plants*. New York, NY: Springer-Verlag, 1989.

SCUDO, F. AND ZIEGLER, J. *The Golden Age of Theoretical Ecology*. New York, NY: Springer-Verlag, 1978.

SMITH, J. MAYNARD. *Models in Ecology*. New York, NY: Cambridge University Press, 1978.

WHITTAKER, R.H. *Communities and Ecosystems*, Second Edition. New York, NY: Macmillan, 1970, 1975.

23.3 Epidemiology

ANDERSON, R.M., ED. *Population Dynamics of Infectious Diseases: Theory and Applications*. New York, NY: Chapman and Hall, 1982.

BAILEY, NORMAN T.J. *The Mathematical Theory of Infectious Diseases and Its Applications*, Second Edition. New York, NY: Macmillan, 1975.

FRAUENTHAL, J.C. *Mathematical Modeling in Epidemiology*. New York, NY: Springer-Verlag, 1980.

23.4 Genetics

* CROW, JAMES R. AND KIMURA, MOTO. *An Introduction to Population Genetics Theory*. New York, NY: Harper and Row, 1970.

EWENS, W.J. *Mathematical Population Genetics*. New York, NY: Springer-Verlag, 1979.

PROVINE, W. *The Origins of Theoretical Population Genetics.* Chicago, IL: University of Chicago Press, 1971.

** SMITH, J. MAYNARD. *Evolution and the Theory of Games.* New York, NY: Cambridge University Press, 1982.

23.5 Population Biology

BROWN, ROBERT L. *Introduction to the Mathematics of Demography.* Winsted, CT: ACTEX Publications, 1991.

** HOPPENSTEADT, FRANK C. *Mathematical Methods of Population Biology.* New York, NY: New York University Press, 1977; New York, NY: Cambridge University Press, 1982.

HOPPENSTEADT, FRANK C. *Mathematical Theories of Populations: Demographics, Genetics, and Epidemics.* Philadelphia, PA: Society for Industrial and Applied Mathematics, 1975.

IMPAGLIAZZO, J. *Deterministic Aspects of Mathematical Demography.* New York, NY: Springer-Verlag, 1985.

*** KEYFITZ, NATHAN AND BEEKMAN, JOHN A. *Demography Through Problems.* New York, NY: Springer-Verlag, 1984.

POLLARD, J.H. *Mathematical Models for the Growth of Human Populations.* New York, NY: Cambridge University Press, 1973.

** SMITH, D.P. AND KEYFITZ, NATHAN. *Mathematical Demography.* New York, NY: Springer-Verlag, 1978.

23.6 Physiology

** BAILAR, JOHN C. AND MOSTELLER, FREDERICK, EDS. *Medical Uses of Statistics.* Waltham, MA: New England Journal of Medicine Books, 1986.

* GLASS, L. AND MACKEY, M.C. *From Clocks to Chaos: The Rhythms of Life.* Princeton, NJ: Princeton University Press, 1988.

* MAZUMDAR, J. *An Introduction to Mathematical Physiology and Biology.* New York, NY: Cambridge University Press, 1989.

SEGEL, LEE A. *Modeling Dynamic Phenomena in Molecular and Cellular Biology.* New York, NY: Cambridge University Press, 1984.

WINFREE, ARTHUR T. *The Geometry of Biological Time,* Second Edition. New York, NY: Springer-Verlag, 1980, 1990.

* WINFREE, ARTHUR T. *The Timing of Biological Clocks.* New York, NY: Scientific American Library, 1987.

24 Applications to Physical Sciences

24.1 General

** ISENBERG, CYRIL. *The Science of Soap Films and Soap Bubbles.* Clevedon: Tieto Ltd., 1978.

LEDERMANN, WALTER AND VAJDA, STEVEN, EDS. *Analysis.* Handbook of Applicable Mathematics, Volume IV. New York, NY: John Wiley, 1982.

* NOBLE, BEN. *Applications of Undergraduate Mathematics in Engineering.* Washington, DC: Mathematical Association of America, 1967.

PEARSON, CARL E., ED. *Handbook of Applied Mathematics: Selected Results and Methods,* Second Edition. New York, NY: Van Nostrand Reinhold, 1974, 1983.

** PÓLYA, GEORGE. *Mathematical Methods in Science.* Washington, DC: Mathematical Association of America, 1977.

* SUTTON, O.G. *Mathematics in Action.* Mineola, NY: Dover, 1966, 1984.

TAUB, A.H., ED. *Studies in Applied Mathematics.* Washington, DC: Mathematical Association of America, 1971.

24.2 Introductory Texts

GREENBERG, MICHAEL D. *Foundations of Applied Mathematics.* Englewood Cliffs, NJ: Prentice Hall, 1978.

KREYSZIG, ERWIN. *Advanced Engineering Mathematics,* Fifth Edition. New York, NY: John Wiley, 1972, 1983.

** STRANG, GILBERT. *Introduction to Applied Mathematics.* Wellesley, MA: Wellesley-Cambridge Press, 1986.

24.3 Advanced Surveys

* COURANT, RICHARD AND HILBERT, DAVID. *Methods of Mathematical Physics,* 2 Vols. New York, NY: John Wiley, 1974, 1989.

JEFFREYS, SIR HAROLD AND JEFFREYS, BERTHA S. *Methods of Mathematical Physics,* Third Edition. New York, NY: Cambridge University Press, 1956.

LIN, C.C. AND SEGEL, LEE A. *Mathematics Applied to Deterministic Problems in the Natural Sciences.* New York, NY: Macmillan, 1974.

REED, MICHAEL AND SIMON, BARRY. *Methods of Modern Mathematical Physics,* 4 Vols. New York, NY: Academic Press, 1972–79.

ZADEH, LOTFI AND DESOER, C.A. *Linear Systems Theory.* New York, NY: McGraw-Hill, 1963.

24.4 Relativity

CLARKE, C. *Elementary General Relativity.* New York, NY: John Wiley, 1979.

* GEROCH, ROBERT. *General Relativity from A to B.* Chicago, IL: University of Chicago Press, 1978.

MISNER, CHARLES W.; THORNE, KIP S.; AND WHEELER, JOHN ARCHIBALD. *Gravitation.* New York, NY: W.H. Freeman, 1973.

24.5 Cosmology and Celestial Mechanics

HOYLE, FRED. *From Stonehenge to Modern Cosmology.* New York, NY: W.H. Freeman, 1972.

* POLLARD, HARRY. *Mathematical Introduction to Celestial Mechanics.* Englewood Cliffs, NJ: Prentice Hall, 1966; Washington, DC: Mathematical Association of America, 1976.

SZEBEHELY, VICTOR G. *Adventures in Celestial Mechanics: A First Course in the Theory of Orbits.* Austin, TX: University of Texas Press, 1989.

WALD, ROBERT M. *Space, Time, and Gravity: The Theory of the Big Bang and Black Holes.* Chicago, IL: University of Chicago Press, 1977.

24.6 Information Theory

CADZOW, JAMES A. *Foundations of Digital Signal Processing and Data Analysis.* New York, NY: Macmillan, 1987.

CHAMBERS, WILLIAM G. *Basics of Communications and Coding.* New York, NY: Oxford University Press, 1985.

JONES, D.S. *Elementary Information Theory.* New York, NY: Clarendon Press, 1979.

* RÉNYI, ALFRÉD. *A Diary on Information Theory.* Budapest: Akademiai Kiado, 1984; New York, NY: John Wiley, 1987.

25 Applications to Social Sciences

25.1 General

DORAN, J.E. AND HODSON, F.R. *Mathematics and Computers in Archaeology.* Cambridge, MA: Harvard University Press, 1975.

GOULD, STEPHEN JAY. *The Mismeasure of Man.* New York, NY: W.W. Norton, 1981.

GROSS, MAURICE. *Mathematical Models in Linguistics.* Englewood Cliffs, NJ: Prentice Hall, 1972.

KEMENY, JOHN G. AND SNELL, J. LAURIE. *Mathematical Models in the Social Sciences.* Cambridge, MA: MIT Press, 1972.

LAZARSFELD, PAUL F., ED. *Mathematical Thinking in the Social Sciences.* New York, NY: Russell and Russell, 1969.

MAKI, DANIEL P. AND THOMPSON, MAYNARD. *Mathematical Models and Applications with Emphasis on the Social, Life, and Management Sciences.* Englewood Cliffs, NJ: Prentice Hall, 1973.

** OLINICK, MICHAEL. *An Introduction to Mathematical Models in the Social and Life Sciences.* Reading, MA: Addison-Wesley, 1978.

RAPOPORT, ANATOL. *Mathematical Models in the Social and Behavioral Sciences.* New York, NY: John Wiley, 1983.

ROBERTS, FRED S. *Graph Theory and Its Applications to Problems of Society.* Philadelphia, PA: Society for Industrial and Applied Mathematics, 1978.

*** TANUR, JUDITH M., *et al.*, EDS. *Statistics: A Guide to Political and Social Issues.* San Francisco, CA: Holden-Day, 1977.

WASHBURN, D.K. AND CROWE, DONALD W. *Symmetries of Culture: Handbook of Plane Pattern Analysis.* Seattle, WA: University of Washington Press, 1988.

25.2 Economics

** BOOT, JOHN C.G. *Common Globe or Global Commons: Population Regulation and Income Distribution.* New York, NY: Marcel Dekker, 1974.

CLARK, COLIN W. *Bioeconomic Modelling and Fisheries Management.* New York, NY: John Wiley, 1985.

* CLARK, COLIN W. *Mathematical Bioeconomics: The Optimal Management of Renewable Resources,* Second Edition. New York, NY: John Wiley, 1976, 1990.

GALE, DAVID. *The Theory of Linear Economic Models.* New York, NY: McGraw-Hill, 1960.

INGRAO, BRUNA AND ISRAEL, GIORGIO. *The Invisible Hand: Economic Equilibrium in the History of Science.* Cambridge, MA: MIT Press, 1990.

KHOURY, SARKIS J. AND PARSONS, TORRENCE D. *Mathematical Methods in Finance and Economics.* New York, NY: Elsevier Science, 1981.

* REITER, STANLEY, ED. *Studies in Mathematical Economics.* Washington, DC: Mathematical Association of America, 1986.

* STARR, ROSS M. *General Equilibrium Models of Monetary Economics: Studies in the Static Foundation of Monetary Theory.* New York, NY: Academic Press, 1989.

VAN DER PLOEG, FREDERICK, ED. *Mathematical Methods in Economics.* New York, NY: John Wiley, 1984.

WONNACOTT, RONALD J. AND WONNACOTT, THOMAS H. *Econometrics,* Second Edition. New York, NY: John Wiley, 1979.

25.3 Political Science

** BALINSKI, MICHAEL L. AND YOUNG, H. PEYTON. *Fair Representation: Meeting the Ideal of One Man, One Vote.* New Haven, CT: Yale University Press, 1982.

BELTRAMI, EDWARD J. *Models for Public Systems Analysis.* New York, NY: Academic Press, 1977.

BRAMS, STEVEN J. AND FISHBURN, PETER C. *Approval Voting.* New York, NY: Birkhäuser, 1983.

** BRAMS, STEVEN J.; LUCAS, WILLIAM F.; AND STRAFFIN, PHILIP D., JR., EDS. *Political and Related Models.* Modules in Applied Mathematics, Vol. 2. New York, NY: Springer-Verlag, 1983.

BRAMS, STEVEN J. *Paradoxes in Politics: An Introduction to the Nonobvious in Political Science.* New York, NY: Free Press, 1976.

BRAMS, STEVEN J. *Superpower Games: Applying Game Theory to Superpower Conflict.* New Haven, CT: Yale University Press, 1985.

STRAFFIN, PHILIP D., JR. *Topics in the Theory of Voting.* New York, NY: Birkhäuser, 1980.

25.4 Psychology

MESSICK, DAVID M., ED. *Mathematical Thinking in Behavioral Sciences,* Readings from Scientific American. New York, NY: W.H. Freeman, 1968.

* TVERSKY, AMOS; COOMBS, CLYDE H.; AND DAWES, ROBYN M. *Mathematical Psychology: An Elementary Introduction.* Englewood Cliffs, NJ: Prentice Hall, 1970.

26 Journals and Periodicals

Journals and periodicals listed below are those that include articles of potential interest to two-year college students and faculty in the mathematical sciences. Titles listed here are devoted primarily to the mathematical sciences. In addition, many general science periodicals such as *Scientific American* and *Sciences News* include excellent articles about the mathematical sciences and should be part of any two-year college library.

*** AMATYC Review
** American Mathematical Monthly
American Statistician
* Arithmetic Teacher
Byte
** Chance
* COMAP Consortium
*** College Mathematics Journal
* Collegiate Microcomputer
Communications of the ACM
Crux Mathematicorum
* Educational Studies in Mathematics
Fibonacci Quarterly
* Historia Mathematica
** Intern. J. of Math. Education in Science and Tech.
Journal for Research in Mathematics Education
* Journal of Recreational Mathematics
Journal of Technology in Mathematics

Journal of Undergraduate Mathematics
* Mathematical Gazette
** Mathematical Intelligencer
Mathematical Spectrum
** Mathematics and Computer Education
Mathematics in College (CUNY)
** Mathematics Magazine
*** Mathematics Teacher
* Notices of the American Mathematical Society
Pentagon
* Pi Mu Epsilon Journal
* Primus
Quantum
* SIAM News
SIAM Review
School Science and Mathematics
** UMAP Journal
*** UME Trends

Index of Authors

A

** Aaboe, Asger. *Episodes from the Early History of Mathematics.* [3.5]

*** Abbott, Edwin A. *Flatland.* [1.5]

* Abelson, Harold. *Turtle Geometry: The Computer as a Medium for Exploring Mathematics.* [14.6]

** ———. *Structure and Interpretation of Computer Programs.* [22.3]

* Adams, Herbert F.R. *Basic Mathematics for Electronics with Calculus.* [16.7]

** ———. *Basic Mathematics for Electronics.* [16.5]

Adams, V. *Affect and Mathematical Problem Solving: A New Perspective.* [5.11]

Adams, William J. *The Life and Times of the Central Limit Theorem.* [3.10]

Ahlfors, Lars V. *Complex Analysis: An Introduction to the Theory of Analytic Functions of One Complex Variable.* [8.4]

*** Aho, Alfred V. *Data Structures and Algorithms.* [22.4]

** ———. *The Design and Analysis of Computer Algorithms.* [22.8]

** ———. *Compilers: Principles, Techniques, and Tools.* [22.13]

Aiton, E.J. *Leibniz: A Biography.* [3.2]

Akhiezer, N.I. *Elements of the Theory of Elliptic Functions.* [8.6]

Albers, Donald J. *International Mathematical Congresses: An Illustrated History, 1893–1986.* [3.6]

*** ———. *Mathematical People: Profiles and Interviews.* [3.2]

———. *Teaching Teachers, Teaching Students: Reflections on Mathematical Education.* [5.6]

*** ———. *More Mathematical People.* [3.2]

** ———. *A Statistical Abstract of Undergraduate Programs in the Mathematical and Computer Sciences, 1990–91.* [5.9]

*** ———. *New Directions in Two-Year College Mathematics.* [5.9]

** Aleksandrov, A.D. *Mathematics: Its Content, Methods, and Meaning.* [1.1]

Alexander, Joyce M. *Thinking With Models: Mathematical Models in the Physical, Biological, and Social Sciences.* [19.2]

Alexanderson, Gerald L. *International Mathematical Congresses: An Illustrated History, 1893–1986.* [3.6]

*** ———. *Mathematical People: Profiles and Interviews.* [3.2]

———. *The William Lowell Putnam Mathematical Competition: Problems and Solutions, 1965–1984.* [4.4]

* ———. *A First Undergraduate Course in Abstract Algebra.* [13.1]

* Alexandroff, Paul. *Elementary Concepts of Topology.* [15.1]

Allenby, R.B.J.T. *Introduction to Number Theory with Computing.* [11.1]

Allendoerfer, C.B. *Principles of Mathematics.* [6.1]

* Althoen, Steven C. *Introduction to Discrete Mathematics.* [10.1]

* American Association for the Advancement of Science. *Science For All Americans.* [5.6]

** American Council of Learned Societies. *Biographical Dictionary of Mathematicians.* [2.3]

Anderson, J.G. *Technical Shop Mathematics.* [16.2]

Anderson, John T. *Excursions in Number Theory.* [11.2]

Anderson, R.M. *Population Dynamics of Infectious Diseases: Theory and Applications.* [23.3]

Andrews, J.G. *Mathematical Modelling.* [19.2]

* Andrews, William S. *Magic Squares and Cubes.* [4.2]

* Anton, Howard. *Applied Finite Mathematics.* [10.2]

———. *Applications of Linear Algebra.* [12.1]

** ———. *Calculus with Analytic Geometry.* [6.3]

** ———. *Elementary Linear Algebra.* [12.1]

Apostol, Tom M. *Selected Papers on Calculus.* [6.5]

———. *Selected Papers on Precalculus.* [6.5]

* ———. *Calculus.* [6.4]

———. *Mathematical Analysis.* [8.2]

Arbib, Michael A. *Brains, Machines, and Mathematics.* [22.11]

Arganbright, Dean E. *Mathematical Applications of Electronic Spreadsheets.* [22.1]

Arnold, V.I. *Huygens and Barrow, Newton and Hooke.* [3.8]

* Arrowsmith, D.K. *An Introduction to Dynamical Systems.* [7.2]

Artin, Emil. *Galois Theory.* [13.5]

Ascher, Marcia. *Code of the Quipu: A Study in Media, Mathematics, and Culture.* [5.4]

* ———. *Ethnomathematics: A Multicultural View of Mathematical Ideas.* [5.4]

Ascher, Robert. *Code of the Quipu: A Study in Media, Mathematics, and Culture.* [5.4]

Ash, Carol. *The Calculus Tutoring Book.* [6.3]

Ash, Robert B. *The Calculus Tutoring Book.* [6.3]

Asimov, Isaac. *Asimov on Numbers.* [1.2]

* Askey, Richard A. *A Century of Mathematics in America.* [3.6]

Athen, Hermann. *Proceedings of the Third International Congress on Mathematical Education.* [5.6]

* Atiyah, Michael F. *Introduction to Commutative Algebra.* [13.6]

Atkinson, Kendall E. *Elementary Numerical Analysis.* [18.1]

Aumann, Robert J. *Handbook of Game Theory with Applications to Economics.* [19.3]

Auslander, Louis. *What Are Numbers?* [6.1]

** Austin, Jacqueline C. *Technical Mathematics.* [16.1]

* Averbach, Bonnie. *Mathematics: Problem Solving through Recreational Mathematics.* [4.1]

* ———. *Applied Finite Mathematics.* [10.2]

B

Baase, Sara. *Computer Algorithms: Introduction to Design and Analysis.* [22.8]

** Bailar, John C. *Medical Uses of Statistics.* [23.6]

Bailey, Norman T.J. *The Mathematical Theory of Infectious Diseases and Its Applications.* [23.3]

Bakel'man, I. Ya. *Inversions.* [14.8]

* Baker, Pauline. *Computer Graphics.* [22.14]

** Balinski, Michael L. *Fair Representation: Meeting the Ideal of One Man, One Vote.* [25.3]

Ball, John E. *Practical Problems in Mathematics for Masons.* [16.2]

*** Ball, W.W. Rouse. *Mathematical Recreations and Essays.* [4.1]

* Banach, Stefan. *Theory of Linear Operators.* [8.5]

Banchoff, Thomas F. *Linear Algebra Through Geometry.* [12.1]

*** ———. *Beyond the Third Dimension: Geometry, Computer Graphics, and Higher Dimensions.* [14.1]

** Barbeau, Edward J. *1001 Problems in High School Mathematics.* [4.4]

———. *Polynomials.* [13.2]

Bard, Allen J. *Chemical Equilibrium.* [16.6]

Barker, Forrest. *Problems in Technical Mathematics for Electricity/Electronics.* [16.5]

Barnett, Raymond A. *Finite Mathematics for Management, Life, and Social Sciences.* [17.2]

*** ———. *Applied Mathematics for Business, Economics, Life Sciences, and Social Sciences.* [17.2]

Barnette, David. *Map Coloring, Polyhedra, and the Four-Color Problem.* [10.4]

*** Barnsley, Michael. *Fractals Everywhere.* [8.3]

* Baron, Margaret E. *The Origins of the Infinitesimal Calculus.* [3.8]

Baroody, A.J. *A Guide to Teaching Mathematics in the Primary Grades.* [5.7]

* Barr, Avron. *The Handbook of Artificial Intelligence.* [22.11]

Barr, Stephen. *Mathematical Brain Benders: 2nd Miscellany of Puzzles.* [4.3]

Bartle, Robert G. *Elements of Real Analysis.* [8.2]

* Barwise, Jon. *The Language of First-Order Logic.* [9.2]

Batastini, Peggy H. *Pharmacological Calculations for Nurses: A Worktext.* [16.3]

Baum, Joan. *The Calculating Passion of Ada Byron.* [3.2]

* Baumgart, John K. *Historical Topics for the Mathematics Classroom.* [5.5]

Beard, R.E. *Risk Theory.* [17.7]

Beatty, William E. *Mathematical Relationships in Business and Economics.* [17.2]

Beauregard, Raymond A. *Linear Algebra.* [12.1]

Beck, Robert E. *Elementary Linear Programming with Applications.* [19.4]

* Beckenbach, Edwin F. *An Introduction to Inequalities.* [8.6]

* Beckmann, Petr. *A History of π(pi).* [3.7]

* Bedini, Silvio. *The Life of Benjamin Banneker.* [3.2]

*** Beekman, John A. *Demography Through Problems.* [23.5]

Behnke, H. *Fundamentals of Mathematics.* [1.1]

Behr, Merlyn. *Number Concepts and Operations in the Middle Grades.* [5.12]

* Beiler, Albert. *Recreations in the Theory of Numbers.* [4.1]

Bell, Eric T. *Mathematics: Queen and Servant of Science.* [1.2]

———. *Men of Mathematics.* [3.2]

Bell, J.L. *A Course in Mathematical Logic.* [9.2]

* Bellman, Richard E. *An Introduction to Inequalities.* [8.6]

Beltrami, Edward J. *Mathematics for Dynamic Modeling.* [19.2]

———. *Models for Public Systems Analysis.* [25.3]

** Bentley, Jon. *More Programming Pearls.* [22.6]

** ———. *Programming Pearls.* [22.6]

Berg, H.C. *Random Walks in Biology.* [23.1]

* Berggren, J.L. *Episodes in the Mathematics of Medieval Islam.* [3.5]

Berkey, Dennis D. *Calculus for Management, Social, and Life Sciences.* [17.4]

Berlekamp, Elwyn R. *Winning Ways for Your Mathematical Plays.* [4.1]

Berlioux, Pierre. *Algorithms: The Construction, Proof, and Analysis of Programs.* [22.8]

Berndt, Bruce C. *Ramanujan's Notebooks.* [3.4]

* Berston, Hyman M. *Collegiate Business Mathematics.* [17.1]

Beth, Evert. *The Foundations of Mathematics.* [9.1]

*** Beyer, William H. *CRC Handbook of Mathematical Sciences.* [2.2]

* ———. *CRC Standard Mathematical Tables and Formulas.* [2.2]

Bidwell, James K. *Readings in the History of Mathematics Education.* [5.5]

* Bierman, Alan. *Great Ideas in Computer Science.* [22.1]

Biggs, Norman L. *Graph Theory, 1736–1936.* [10.4]

Billingsley, Patrick. *Probability and Measure.* [20.6]

Billstein, Rick. *Logo.* [14.6]

** Bing, R.H. *Elementary Point Set Topology.* [15.1]

*** Birkhoff, Garrett. *A Survey of Modern Algebra.* [13.1]

———. *Ordinary Differential Equations.* [7.2]

———. *Algebra.* [13.2]

Bishop, Alan J. *Mathematical Enculturation: A Cultural Perspective on Mathematics Education.* [5.4]

** Bittinger, Marvin L. *Finite Mathematics.* [10.2]

** ———. *Mathematics and Calculus with Applications.* [17.4]

———. *Applied Calculus.* [17.4]

** ———. *Business Mathematics for College Students.* [17.1]

———. *Calculus: A Modeling Approach.* [6.3]

* Blackwell, David. *Mathematics: Report of the Project 2061 Phase I Mathematics Panel.* [5.6]

Bleloch, Andrew L. *How to Model It: Problem Solving for the Computer Age.* [19.2]

Bliss, Elizabeth. *Data Processing Mathematics.* [16.4]

* Blumenthal, Leonard M. *Modern View of Geometry.* [14.8]

* Bochner, Salomon. *The Role of Mathematics in the Rise of Science.* [1.3]

Boehm, George A.W. *The Mathematical Sciences: A Collection of Essays.* [1.1]

Bogart, Kenneth P. *Introductory Combinatorics.* [10.3]

Boisen, M.B., Jr. *Calculus with Applications.* [17.4]

* Boisselle, A.H. *Business Mathematics Today.* [17.1]

Bold, Benjamin. *Famous Problems of Geometry and How to Solve Them.* [14.1]

* Bolter, J. David. *Turing's Man: Western Culture in the Computer Age.* [22.2]

** Bondy, J. Adrian. *Graph Theory with Applications.* [10.4]

Bonola, Roberto. *Non-Euclidean Geometry: A Critical and Historical Study of Its Development.* [3.9]

* Boole, George. *An Investigation of the Laws of Thought.* [9.2]

* ———. *Treatise on the Calculus of Finite Differences.* [3.4]

** Boot, John C.G. *Common Globe or Global Commons: Population Regulation and Income Distribution.* [25.2]

* Borwein, Jonathan M. *A Dictionary of Real Numbers.* [2.2]

* Borwein, Peter B. *A Dictionary of Real Numbers.* [2.2]

Bottazzini, Umberto. *The Higher Calculus: A History of Real and Complex Analysis from Euler to Weierstrass.* [3.8]

Bowden, Leon. *The Role of Mathematics in Science.* [1.3]

*** Bowen, Earl K. *Mathematics with Applications in Management and Economics.* [17.6]

*** Bowers, Newton L., Jr. *Actuarial Mathematics.* [17.7]

* Box, George E.P. *Statistics for Experimenters: An Introduction to Design, Data Analysis, and Model Building.* [21.4]

Box, Joan Fisher. *R.A. Fisher: The Life of a Scientist.* [3.2]

* Boyce, John B. *Mathematics for Technical and Vocational Students.* [16.2]

*** Boyce, William E. *Elementary Differential Equations and Boundary Value Problems.* [7.1]

———. *Case Studies in Mathematical Modeling.* [19.2]

*** Boyer, Carl B. *A History of Mathematics.* [3.1]

* ———. *History of Analytic Geometry.* [3.9]

** ———. *The History of Calculus and Its Conceptual Development.* [3.8]

Bradford, Robert. *Mathematics for Carpenters.* [16.2]

Bradley, Gerald L. *Calculus for Business, Economics, and the Social and Life Sciences.* [17.4]

Bradley, J.G. *Shop Mathematics.* [16.2]

Bram, Joseph. *Nonlinear Mathematics.* [19.5]

Brams, Steven J. *Approval Voting.* [25.3]

———. *Game Theory and National Security.* [19.3]

** ———. *Political and Related Models.* [25.3]

———. *Paradoxes in Politics: An Introduction to the Nonobvious in Political Science.* [25.3]

———. *Superpower Games: Applying Game Theory to Superpower Conflict.* [25.3]

Brandreth, Gyles. *Numberplay.* [4.2]

Brassard, Gilles. *Algorithmics: Theory and Practice.* [22.8]

Bratley, Paul. *A Guide to Simulation.* [19.5]

———. *Algorithmics: Theory and Practice.* [22.8]

** Braun, Martin. *Differential Equation Models.* [19.2]

———. *Differential Equations and Their Applications: An Introduction to Applied Mathematics.* [7.1]

Brawer, Steven. *Introduction to Parallel Programming.* [22.6]

* Brenna, L.V. *Business Mathematics Today.* [17.1]

Bressoud, David M. *Factorization and Primality Testing.* [11.4]

* ———. *Second Year Calculus.* [6.4]

Brewer, James W. *Emmy Noether: A Tribute to Her Life and Work.* [3.2]

Brieskorn, Egbert. *Plane Algebraic Curves.* [14.7]

* Bronshtein, I.N. *Handbook of Mathematics.* [2.2]

Brook, Richard J. *The Fascination of Statistics.* [21.1]

** Broverman, Samuel A. *Mathematics of Investment and Finance.* [17.5]

* Brown, James W. *Fourier Series and Boundary Value Problems.* [7.2]

* Brown, Richard H. *Artificial Intelligence: An MIT Perspective.* [22.11]

Brown, Robert L. *Mathematics of Finance.* [17.5]

———. *Introduction to the Mathematics of Demography.* [23.5]

Brown, Stephen I. *The Art of Problem Posing.* [5.11]

Bruce, J.W. *Microcomputers and Mathematics.* [22.1]

Buck, R. Creighton. *Advanced Calculus.* [6.4]

Buckley, Fred. *Distance in Graphs.* [10.4]

** Budden, F.J. *The Fascination of Groups.* [13.3]

Budnick, Frank S. *Applied Mathematics for Business, Economics, and the Social Sciences.* [17.2]

** Bühler, Walter K. *Gauss: A Biographical Study.* [3.2]

Buhlman, Hans. *Mathematical Methods in Risk Theory.* [17.7]

* Bumcrot, Robert J. *Introduction to Discrete Mathematics.* [10.1]

Bunch, Bryan H. *Mathematical Fallacies and Paradoxes.* [1.2]

** Burden, Richard L. *Numerical Analysis.* [18.1]

Burger, Dionys. *Sphereland.* [14.1]

Burgmeier, J.W. *Calculus with Applications.* [17.4]

Burington, Richard S. *Handbook of Probability and Statistics with Tables.* [2.2]

*** Burke, Charles J. *Applied Mathematics for Business, Economics, Life Sciences, and Social Sciences.* [17.2]

Burks, Alice R. *The First Electronic Computer: The Atanasoff Story.* [3.2]

Burks, Arthur W. *The First Electronic Computer: The Atanasoff Story.* [3.2]

Burn, R.P. *Groups: A Path to Geometry.* [13.3]

Burns, Marilyn. *The I Hate Mathematics! Book.* [5.7]

Burton, David M. *The History of Mathematics: An Introduction.* [3.1]

Burton, Leone. *Thinking Mathematically.* [5.11]

Butcher, Marjorie V. *Mathematics of Compound Interest.* [17.5]

C

Cacoullos, T. *Exercises in Probability.* [20.1]

Cadzow, James A. *Foundations of Digital Signal Processing and Data Analysis.* [24.6]

** Cajori, Florian. *A History of Mathematical Notations.* [3.1]

———. *A History of Mathematics.* [3.1]

Calinger, Ronald. *Classics of Mathematics.* [3.3]

Calter, Paul. *Mathematics for Computer Technology.* [16.4]

** ———. *Technical Mathematics with Calculus.* [16.7]

Campbell, Douglas M. *Mathematics: People, Problems, Results.* [1.1]

** Campbell, Paul J. *Mathematics Education in Secondary Schools and Two-Year Colleges: A Sourcebook.* [5.8]

* ———. *Women of Mathematics: A Biobibliographic Sourcebook.* [5.10]

* Cardano, Girolamo. *The Great Art or the Rules of Algebra.* [3.4]

Carlo, Patrick. *Merchandising Mathematics.* [16.2]

Carman, Robert A. *Mathematics for the Trades: A Guided Approach.* [16.2]

Carolan, Mary Jane. *Clinical Calculations for Nurses.* [16.3]

* Carroll, Lewis. *Mathematical Recreations of Lewis Carroll.* [4.2]

Carss, Marjorie. *Proceedings of the Fifth International Congress on Mathematical Education.* [5.6]

* Casti, John L. *Alternate Realities: Mathematical Models of Nature and Man.* [23.1]

* Casualty Actuarial Society. *Foundations of Casualty Actuarial Science.* [17.7]

Casulli, Vincenzo. *Numerical Analysis for Applied Mathematics, Science, and Engineering.* [18.2]

Cederberg, Judith N. *A Course in Modern Geometries.* [14.2]

* Chace, Arnold B. *The Rhind Mathematical Papyrus.* [3.4]

Chambers, John M. *Graphical Methods for Data Analysis.* [21.5]

Chambers, William G. *Basics of Communications and Coding.* [24.6]

Chang, C.C. *Model Theory.* [9.4]

* Charles, Randall I. *The Teaching and Assessing of Mathematical Problem Solving.* [5.12]

———. *How To Evaluate Progress in Problem Solving.* [5.11]

Chartrand, Gary. *Introductory Graph Theory.* [10.4]

Chatfield, Christopher. *Problem Solving: A Statistician's Guide.* [21.3]

* Chazan, Daniel. *How to Use Conjecturing and Microcomputers to Teach Geometry.* [5.14]

* Chein, Orin. *Mathematics: Problem Solving through Recreational Mathematics.* [4.1]

Cheney, Elliot W. *Numerical Mathematics and Computing.* [18.1]

———. *Introduction to Approximation Theory.* [18.4]

** ———. *Numerical Analysis: Mathematics of Scientific Computing.* [18.1]

* Childs, Lindsay. *A Concrete Introduction to Higher Algebra.* [13.1]

*** Chinn, William G. *First Concepts of Topology.* [15.1]

———. *3.1416 And All That.* [1.6]

Chrystal, George. *Textbook of Algebra.* [3.4]

** Chung, Kai Lai. *Elementary Probability Theory with Stochastic Processes.* [20.2]

* Churchill, Ruel V. *Fourier Series and Boundary Value Problems.* [7.2]

** Chvátal, Vasek. *Linear Programming.* [19.4]

** Cipra, Barry. *Misteaks ... and How to Find Them Before the Teacher Does ....* [6.5]

* Cissell, H. *Mathematics of Finance.* [17.5]

* Cissell, R. *Mathematics of Finance.* [17.5]

Clark, Colin W. *Bioeconomic Modelling and Fisheries Management.* [25.2]

———. *Dynamic Modeling in Behavioral Ecology.* [23.2]

* ———. *Mathematical Bioeconomics: The Optimal Management of Renewable Resources.* [25.2]

** Clark, Frank J. *Mathematics for Programming Computers.* [16.4]

Clarke, C. *Elementary General Relativity.* [24.4]

Clason, Robert G. *Readings in the History of Mathematics Education.* [5.5]

Clayson, J. *Visual Modeling with Logo.* [14.6]

Cleaves, Cheryl. *Introduction to Technical Mathematics.* [16.1]

* ———. *Basic Mathematics for Trades and Technologies.* [16.2]

** Clemens, Stanley R. *Geometry: An Investigative Approach.* [14.3]

* Cleveland, William S. *The Elements of Graphing Data.* [21.5]

* Clocksin, W.F. *Programming in Prolog.* [22.7]

Closs, Michael P. *Native American Mathematics.* [5.4]

Cochran, William G. *Sampling Techniques.* [21.7]

** ———. *Statistical Methods.* [21.4]

Cocking, R.R. *Linguistic and Cultural Influences on Learning Mathematics.* [5.4]

** Coddington, Earl A. *Theory of Ordinary Differential Equations.* [7.2]

Cohen, Daniel I.A. *Basic Techniques of Combinatorial Theory.* [10.3]

Cohen, David. *Precalculus.* [6.2]

Cohen, Patricia Cline. *A Calculating People: The Spread of Numeracy in Early America.* [5.5]

* Cohen, Paul R. *The Handbook of Artificial Intelligence.* [22.11]

** Cohn-Vossen, S. *Geometry and the Imagination.* [14.1]

** Coleman, Courtney S. *Differential Equation Models.* [19.2]

 * Committee on Mathematical Education of Teachers. *Guidelines for the Continuing Mathematical Education of Teachers.* [5.6]

** Committee on the Undergraduate Program in Mathematics. *Reshaping College Mathematics.* [5.9]

Conference Board of the Mathematical Sciences. *Overview and Analysis of School Mathematics, Grades K–12.* [5.6]

** Consortium for Mathematics. *For All Practical Purposes: Introduction to Contemporary Mathematics.* [1.4]

Conte, Samuel D. *Elementary Numerical Analysis: An Algorithmic Approach.* [18.1]

Conway, John Horton. *Winning Ways for Your Mathematical Plays.* [4.1]

 * ——. *On Numbers and Games.* [10.3]

 * Cooke, Nelson M. *Basic Mathematics for Electronics with Calculus.* [16.7]

** ——. *Basic Mathematics for Electronics.* [16.5]

 * Cooke, William P. *Quantitative Methods for Management Decisions.* [17.6]

 * Coolidge, Julian L. *A History of the Conic Sections and Quadric Surfaces.* [3.9]

——. *The Mathematics of Great Amateurs.* [3.1]

 * Coombs, Clyde H. *Mathematical Psychology: An Elementary Introduction.* [25.4]

 * Cooney, Thomas J. *Perspectives on Research on Effective Mathematics Teaching.* [5.12]

** ——. *Teaching and Learning Mathematics in the 1990s: 1990 Yearbook.* [5.6]

 * Cooper, D. *Standard Pascal: User Reference Manual.* [22.7]

Cooper, J. *Mathematics of Accounting.* [17.5]

Cooper, Necia G. *From Cardinals to Chaos: Reflections on the Life and Legacy of Stanislaw Ulam.* [3.2]

 * Courant, Richard. *Methods of Mathematical Physics.* [24.3]

——. *Introduction to Calculus and Analysis.* [6.4]

** ——. *What is Mathematics?* [1.2]

——. *Differential and Integral Calculus.* [6.4]

Cowles, Michael. *Statistics in Psychology: An Historical Perspective.* [3.10]

Cox, Brad J. *Object-Oriented Programming: An Evolutionary Approach.* [22.6]

Coxeter, H.S.M. *M.C. Escher: Art and Science.* [14.5]

 * ——. *Geometry Revisited.* [14.4]

*** ——. *Introduction to Geometry.* [14.2]

*** ——. *Mathematical Recreations and Essays.* [4.1]

Coxford, Arthur F. *Advanced Mathematics: A Preparation for Calculus.* [6.2]

 * ——. *The Ideas of Algebra, K–12: 1988 Yearbook.* [5.8]

Craig, Allen T. *Introduction to Mathematical Statistics.* [21.4]

Cross, Mark. *Learning the Art of Mathematical Modelling.* [19.2]

 * Crow, James R. *An Introduction to Population Genetics Theory.* [23.4]

Crowe, Donald W. *Symmetries of Culture: Handbook of Plane Pattern Analysis.* [25.1]

Crowell, Richard H. *Calculus of Vector Functions.* [6.4]

Crowley, Michael F. *Women and Minorities in Science and Engineering.* [5.10]

** Crown, J. Conrad. *Finite Mathematics.* [10.2]

** ——. *Mathematics and Calculus with Applications.* [17.4]

Crump, Thomas. *The Anthropology of Numbers.* [3.7]

Cullen, Michael R. *Mathematics for the Biosciences.* [23.1]

** Cunningham, Steve. *Visualization in Teaching and Learning Mathematics.* [5.9]

Curtis, A.B. *Mathematics of Accounting.* [17.5]

D

D'Abrera, H.J.M. *Nonparametrics: Statistical Methods Based on Ranks.* [21.8]

Dahl, O.J. *Structured Programming.* [22.6]

 * Daintith, John. *The Penguin Dictionary of Mathematics.* [2.1]

Dalton, LeRoy C. *Topics for Mathematics Clubs.* [5.8]

Daniel, James W. *Applied Linear Algebra.* [12.1]

Daniels, Jeanne M. *Clinical Calculations: A Unified Approach.* [16.3]

 * Dantzig, George B. *Studies in Optimization.* [19.1]

 * ——. *Linear Programming and Extensions.* [19.4]

Dantzig, Tobias. *Number, The Language of Science.* [1.2]

 * Date, C.J. *An Introduction to Database Systems.* [22.5]

Dauben, Joseph W. *Mathematical Perspectives: Essays on Mathematics and Its Historical Development.* [3.6]

——. *Georg Cantor: His Mathematics and Philosophy of the Infinite.* [3.2]

 * ——. *The History of Mathematics from Antiquity to the Present: A Selective Bibliography.* [2.4]

 * Davenport, Harold. *The Higher Arithmetic: An Introduction to the Theory of Numbers.* [11.1]

Davenport, J.H. *Computer Algebra: Systems and Algorithms for Algebraic Computation.* [22.8]

 * David, F.N. *Games, Gods, and Gambling.* [20.1]

Davidson, Judy K. *Pharmacological Calculations for Nurses: A Worktext.* [16.3]

 * Davidson, Neil. *Cooperative Learning in Mathematics: A Handbook for Teachers.* [5.6]

Davis, Dennis D. *Practical Problems in Mathematics for Machinists.* [16.2]

*** Davis, Howard T. *Fundamental Mathematics for Health Careers.* [16.3]

Davis, Linda. *Technical Mathematics with Calculus.* [16.7]

Davis, Martin D. *Computability, Complexity, and Languages: Fundamentals of Theoretical Computer Science.* [22.9]

** Davis, Monte. *Catastrophe Theory.* [19.2]

Davis, Morton D. *Game Theory: A Nontechnical Introduction.* [19.3]
* Davis, Philip F. *Methods of Numerical Integration.* [18.1]
Davis, Philip J. *3.1416 And All That.* [1.6]
* ———. *Descartes' Dream: The World According to Mathematics.* [1.2]
* ———. *The Mathematical Experience.* [1.2]
———. *Interpolation and Approximation.* [18.4]
———. *The Lore of Large Numbers.* [11.3]
* Davis, Ronald M. *A Curriculum in Flux: Mathematics at Two-Year Colleges.* [5.9]
* Dawes, Robyn M. *Mathematical Psychology: An Elementary Introduction.* [25.4]
de Boor, Carl. *Elementary Numerical Analysis: An Algorithmic Approach.* [18.1]
* De Mestre, Neville. *The Mathematics of Projectiles in Sport.* [6.5]
* Decker, Rick. *The Analytical Engine.* [22.1]
* Dedekind, Richard. *Essays on the Theory of Numbers.* [3.4]
DeGroot, Morris H. *Statistics and the Law.* [21.1]
Deitel, Barbara. *Computers and Data Processing.* [16.4]
Deitel, Harvey M. *Computers and Data Processing.* [16.4]
* ———. *Operating Systems.* [22.10]
deKryger, William J. *Math for the Automotive Trade.* [16.2]
* Dell, Peter B. *Basic Mathematics for Electronics with Calculus.* [16.7]
** ———. *Basic Mathematics for Electronics.* [16.5]
Demana, Franklin D. *Transition to College Mathematics.* [6.2]
** ———. *Precalculus Mathematics—A Graphing Approach.* [6.2]
*** ———. *Graphing Calculator and Computer Graphing Laboratory Manual.* [6.2]
* Deming, W. Edwards. *Out of The Crisis.* [21.1]
———. *Some Theory of Sampling.* [21.7]
Denes, J. *Latin Squares and Their Applications.* [10.3]
* Deo, Narsingh. *Combinatorial Algorithms: Theory and Practice.* [22.8]
Desoer, C.A. *Linear Systems Theory.* [24.3]
* Devaney, Robert L. *Chaos and Fractals: The Mathematics Behind the Computer Graphics.* [8.3]
———. *An Introduction to Chaotic Dynamical Systems.* [8.3]
*** ———. *Chaos, Fractals, and Dynamics: Computer Experiments in Mathematics.* [8.3]
Devlin, Keith J. *Fundamentals of Contemporary Set Theory.* [9.3]
———. *Mathematics: The New Golden Age.* [1.2]
Devore, Jay L. *Statistics: The Exploration and Analysis of Data.* [21.2]
———. *Probability and Statistics for Engineering and the Sciences.* [21.4]
* DeVore, Russell. *Practical Problems in Mathematics for Heating and Cooling Technicians.* [16.2]
*** Dewdney, A.K. *The Armchair Universe: An Exploration of Computer Worlds.* [22.1]

* ———. *The Planiverse.* [1.5]
*** ———. *The Turing Omnibus: 61 Excursions in Computer Science.* [22.1]
* Diamond, H.G. *The Theory of Algebraic Numbers.* [11.5]
* Dick, Auguste. *Emmy Noether, 1882–1935.* [3.2]
** Dickson, Leonard E. *History of the Theory of Numbers.* [3.7]
Dietrich, Frank H. *Statistics.* [21.2]
Dieudonné, Jean. *Abrégé d'histoire des Mathématiques, 1700–1900.* [3.1]
** Dijksterhuis, E.J. *Archimedes.* [3.4]
Dijkstra, Edsger W. *Structured Programming.* [22.6]
———. *A Discipline of Programming.* [22.6]
*** DiPrima, Richard C. *Elementary Differential Equations and Boundary Value Problems.* [7.1]
* diSessa, Andrea A. *Turtle Geometry: The Computer as a Medium for Exploring Mathematics.* [14.6]
Doerr, Alan. *Applied Discrete Structures for Computer Science.* [10.1]
Domoryad, A.P. *Mathematical Games and Pastimes.* [4.2]
Doran, J.E. *Mathematics and Computers in Archaeology.* [25.1]
Dornhoff, Larry L. *Applied Modern Algebra.* [13.1]
Dörrie, Heinrich. *100 Great Problems of Elementary Mathematics.* [1.3]
Dossey, John A. *Discrete Mathematics.* [10.1]
** ———. *The Mathematics Report Card: Are We Measuring Up?* [5.13]
*** Douglas, Ronald G. *Toward A Lean and Lively Calculus.* [5.9]
Downs, Floyd L. *Geometry.* [14.3]
Doyle, Peter G. *Random Walks and Electric Networks.* [20.4]
Draper, Norman R. *Applied Regression Analysis.* [21.6]
** Drew, Donald A. *Differential Equation Models.* [19.2]
Dù Shírán. *Chinese Mathematics: A Concise History.* [3.5]
Dubins, Lester E. *Inequalities for Stochastic Processes (How to Gamble If You Must).* [20.4]
Dudeney, Henry E. *536 Puzzles and Curious Problems.* [4.3]
———. *Amusements in Mathematics.* [4.3]
Dudenhefer, Paul. *Introduction to Technical Mathematics.* [16.1]
** Dudley, Underwood. *A Budget of Trisections.* [14.4]
———. *Elementary Number Theory.* [11.1]
*** Dunham, William. *Journey Through Genius: The Great Theorems of Mathematics.* [1.4]
* Duren, Peter. *A Century of Mathematics in America.* [3.6]
Durrett, Richard. *Probability: Theory and Examples.* [20.3]

E

Earle, James. *Geometry for Engineers.* [16.7]
Easterday, Kenneth E. *Activities for Junior High School and Middle School Mathematics.* [5.8]

* Eaves, B.C. *Studies in Optimization.* [19.1]
* Edelstein-Keshet, Leah. *Mathematical Models in Biology.* [23.1]
* Edwards, A.W.F. *Pascal's Arithmetical Triangle.* [3.5]
* Edwards, C.H., Jr. *Elementary Differential Equations with Applications.* [7.1]
*** ———. *The Historical Development of the Calculus.* [3.8]
  Edwards, Harold M. *Fermat's Last Theorem: A Genetic Introduction to Algebraic Number Theory.* [11.5]
  Efron, Bradley. *The Jackknife, the Bootstrap, and Other Resampling Plans.* [21.5]
  Eggen, M. *A Transition to Advanced Mathematics.* [8.1]
  Ellis, A.J. *Basic Algebra and Geometry for Scientists and Engineers.* [16.7]
  Enderton, Herbert B. *A Mathematical Introduction to Logic.* [9.2]
  ———. *Elements of Set Theory.* [9.3]
  ———. *Linear Algebra.* [12.1]
  Epp, Susanna S. *Discrete Mathematics with Applications.* [10.1]
  Ernest, Paul. *The Philosophy of Mathematics Education.* [5.2]
  Ernst, John F. *Basic Technical Mathematics with Calculus.* [16.7]
* Etchemendy, John. *The Language of First-Order Logic.* [9.2]
  Euler, Leonhard. *Introduction to Analysis of the Infinite.* [3.4]
** Eves, Howard W. *A Survey of Geometry.* [14.2]
*** ———. *An Introduction to the History of Mathematics with Cultural Connections.* [3.1]
** ———. *Foundations and Fundamental Concepts of Mathematics.* [9.1]
* ———. *Great Moments in Mathematics (After 1650).* [3.6]
* ———. *Great Moments in Mathematics (Before 1650).* [3.5]
* ———. *Mathematical Circles.* [1.5]
*** Ewen, Dale. *Elementary Technical Mathematics.* [16.1]
* ———. *Mathematics for Technical Education.* [16.7]
* ———. *Technical Calculus.* [16.7]
  Ewens, W.J. *Mathematical Population Genetics.* [23.4]

F

  Fadiman, Clifton. *Fantasia Mathematica.* [1.5]
  ———. *The Mathematical Magpie.* [1.5]
** Faires, J. Douglas. *Numerical Analysis.* [18.1]
  Farlow, Stanley J. *Applied Mathematics for Business, Economics, and the Social Sciences.* [17.2]
  ———. *Calculus and Its Applications.* [17.4]
** Fauvel, John. *The History of Mathematics: A Reader.* [3.1]
* Feigenbaum, Edward A. *The Handbook of Artificial Intelligence.* [22.11]

  Felker, C.A. *Shop Mathematics.* [16.2]
** Feller, William. *An Introduction to Probability Theory and Its Applications.* [20.3]
** Fennema, Elizabeth. *Mathematics and Gender.* [5.10]
  Fey, James T. *Computing and Mathematics: The Impact on Secondary School Curricula.* [5.14]
  Fienberg, Stephen E. *Beginning Statistics with Data Analysis.* [21.5]
  ———. *Statistics and the Law.* [21.1]
  Finney, Ross L. *Calculus.* [6.3]
*** ———. *Calculus and Analytic Geometry.* [6.3]
** Firby, P.A. *Surface Topology.* [15.2]
  Fischer, Charles N. *Crafting a Compiler.* [22.13]
  Fishburn, Peter C. *Approval Voting.* [25.3]
* Fisher, Paul. *Collegiate Business Mathematics.* [17.1]
  Fisher, Ronald A. *Statistical Methods, Experimental Design, and Scientific Inference.* [21.8]
  Fishman, G.S. *Principles of Discrete Event Simulation.* [19.5]
  Fiume, Eugene L. *The Mathematical Structure of Raster Graphics.* [22.14]
* Flaspohler, D. *Mathematics of Finance.* [17.5]
* Fleck, George. *Shaping Space: A Polyhedral Approach.* [14.5]
  Foerster, Paul A. *Precalculus with Trigonometry: Functions and Applications.* [6.2]
** Foley, James D. *Computer Graphics: Principles and Practice.* [22.14]
  Fomenko, Anatoliĭ T. *Mathematical Impressions.* [1.6]
  Fomin, S.V. *Introductory Real Analysis.* [8.2]
* Ford, Wendy W. *The Psychology of Mathematics for Instruction.* [5.3]
  Forrester, Robert P. *Mathematics for the Allied Health Professions.* [16.3]
*** Forster, H. *Basic Mathematics for Electricity and Electronics.* [16.5]
  Fox, Bennett L. *A Guide to Simulation.* [19.5]
  Fraenkel, Abraham A. *Abstract Set Theory.* [9.3]
  Fraleigh, John B. *Linear Algebra.* [12.1]
  Francis, George K. *A Topological Picturebook.* [15.2]
  Frauenthal, J.C. *Mathematical Modeling in Epidemiology.* [23.3]
** Freedman, David. *Statistics.* [21.2]
* Freeman, D.M. *Business Mathematics Today.* [17.1]
  Freiberger, Paul. *Fire in the Valley: The Making of the Personal Computer.* [3.11]
  French, Simon. *Readings in Decision Analysis.* [19.1]
  Freudenthal, Hans. *Mathematics as an Educational Task.* [5.2]
  Fröberg, Carl-Erik. *Numerical Mathematics: Theory and Computer Applications.* [18.5]
  Fulton, William. *Algebraic Curves: An Introduction to Algebraic Geometry.* [14.7]

G

  Gaal, Lisl. *Classical Galois Theory with Examples.* [13.5]

** Gaffney, Matthew P. *Annotated Bibliography of Expository Writing in the Mathematical Sciences.* [2.4]

Gale, David. *The Theory of Linear Economic Models.* [25.2]

* Galilei, Galileo. *Dialogues Concerning Two New Sciences.* [3.4]

* Gallian, Joseph A. *Contemporary Abstract Algebra.* [13.1]

Gallin, Daniel. *Applied Mathematics for the Management, Life, and Social Sciences.* [17.2]

Gani, J. *The Craft of Probabilistic Modelling: A Collection of Personal Accounts.* [20.1]

————. *The Making of Statisticians.* [3.10]

** Gardiner, A. *Discovering Mathematics: The Art of Investigation.* [1.4]

————. *Mathematical Puzzling.* [4.6]

** Gardiner, C.F. *Surface Topology.* [15.2]

Gårding, Lars. *Encounter with Mathematics.* [1.2]

*** Gardner, Martin. *The Mathematical Puzzles of Sam Loyd.* [4.3]

————. *Aha! Gotcha.* [4.5]

————. *Aha! Insight.* [4.5]

* ————. *Hexaflexagons and Other Mathematical Diversions.* [4.5]

* ————. *Knotted Doughnuts and Other Mathematical Entertainments.* [4.5]

* ————. *Martin Gardner's New Mathematical Diversions from Scientific American.* [4.5]

————. *Mathematical Carnival.* [4.5]

* ————. *Mathematical Magic Show.* [4.5]

* ————. *Penrose Tiles to Trapdoor Ciphers.* [4.5]

* ————. *Riddles of the Sphinx And Other Mathematical Puzzle Tales.* [4.5]

————. *Science Fiction Puzzle Tales.* [4.5]

* ————. *The Magic Numbers of Dr. Matrix.* [4.5]

————. *Time Travel and Other Mathematical Bewilderments.* [4.5]

————. *Wheels, Life, and Other Mathematical Amusements.* [4.5]

* Garey, Michael R. *Computers and Intractability: A Guide to the Theory of NP-Completeness.* [22.9]

* Garrad, Crawford G. *Practical Problems in Mathematics for Electricians.* [16.2]

Garrett, Leonard J. *Data Structures, Algorithms, and Program Style Using C.* [22.4]

* Gass, Saul I. *Decision Making, Models, and Algorithms: A First Course.* [19.1]

————. *Linear Programming: Methods and Applications.* [19.4]

Gause, G.F. *The Struggle for Existence.* [23.2]

Gazis, Denos C. *Traffic Science.* [19.5]

Geis, I. *How to Lie with Statistics.* [21.1]

————. *How to Take a Chance.* [20.1]

*** Gelbaum, Bernard R. *Theorems and Counterexamples in Mathematics.* [8.2]

*** Gellert, Walter. *The VNR Concise Encyclopedia of Mathematics.* [2.3]

Gerald, Curtis F. *Applied Numerical Analysis.* [18.1]

* Geroch, Robert. *General Relativity from A to B.* [24.4]

*** Gerstein, Larry J. *Discrete Mathematics and Algebraic Structures.* [10.1]

Giblin, P.J. *Microcomputers and Mathematics.* [22.1]

————. *Graphs, Surfaces and Homology: An Introduction to Algebraic Topology.* [15.3]

** Gigerenzer, Gerd. *The Empire of Chance: How Probability Changed Science and Everyday Life.* [3.10]

** Gill, Jack C. *Technical Mathematics.* [16.1]

Gillings, Richard J. *Mathematics in the Times of the Pharaohs.* [3.5]

* Gillispie, Charles C. *Dictionary of Scientific Biography.* [2.3]

* Giordano, Frank R. *A First Course in Mathematical Modeling.* [19.2]

* Glass, L. *From Clocks to Chaos: The Rhythms of Life.* [23.6]

Glassner, Andrew. *Graphics Gems.* [22.14]

————. *An Introduction to Ray Tracing.* [22.14]

* Gleason, Andrew M. *The William Lowell Putnam Mathematical Competition: Problems and Solutions, 1938–1964.* [4.4]

*** Gleick, James. *Chaos: Making a New Science.* [1.2]

Glynn, Jerry. *Exploring Mathematics with Mathematica: Dialogs Concerning Computers and Mathematics.* [22.1]

** Gnanadesikan, Mrudulla. *The Art and Techniques of Simulation.* [20.1]

Gnedenko, Boris V. *An Elementary Introduction to the Theory of Probability.* [20.2]

————. *The Theory of Probability and the Elements of Statistics.* [20.3]

Goetsch, David L. *Mathematics for the Automotive Trades.* [16.2]

————. *Mathematics for the Heating, Ventilating, and Cooling Trades.* [16.2]

————. *Mathematics for the Machine Trades.* [16.2]

Goffman, Casper. *A First Course in Functional Analysis.* [8.5]

Goldberg, Adele. *Smalltalk-80: The Language.* [22.7]

** Goldberg, Samuel I. *Introduction to Difference Equations.* [10.5]

** Goldfish, Dorothy M. *Basic Mathematics for Beginning Chemistry.* [16.6]

* Goldstein, Larry J. *Calculus and Its Applications.* [6.3]

* ————. *Finite Mathematics and Its Applications.* [10.2]

* Goldstine, Herman H. *The Computer from Pascal to von Neumann.* [3.11]

** Golomb, Solomon W. *Polyominoes.* [4.6]

Golos, Ellery B. *Patterns in Mathematics.* [1.4]

* Golub, Gene H. *Matrix Computations.* [18.3]

————. *Studies in Numerical Analysis.* [18.2]

Good, I.J. *Good Thinking: The Foundations of Probability and Its Applications.* [20.5]

Goodson, C.E. *Technical Mathematics with Calculus.* [16.7]

Goos, Gerhard. *Compiler Construction.* [22.13]

Goritz, John. *Mathematics for Welding Trades.* [16.2]

Gould, Stephen Jay. *The Mismeasure of Man.* [25.1]

Gowar, Norman. *An Invitation to Mathematics.* [1.4]

Grabiner, Judith V. *The Origins of Cauchy's Rigorous Calculus.* [3.8]

Graham, L.A. *Ingenious Mathematical Problems and Methods.* [4.4]

** Graham, Ronald L. *Concrete Mathematics: A Foundation for Computer Science.* [10.3]

Grandine, Thomas A. *The Numerical Methods Programming Projects Book.* [18.5]

** Gray, Jeremy. *The History of Mathematics: A Reader.* [3.1]

Gray, Theodore W. *Exploring Mathematics with Mathematica: Dialogs Concerning Computers and Mathematics.* [22.1]

Greenberg, Marvin Jay. *Lectures on Algebraic Topology.* [15.3]

——. *Euclidean and Non-Euclidean Geometries: Development and History.* [14.4]

Greenberg, Michael D. *Foundations of Applied Mathematics.* [24.2]

Greenspan, Donald. *Numerical Analysis for Applied Mathematics, Science, and Engineering.* [18.2]

* Greenwood, R.E. *The William Lowell Putnam Mathematical Competition: Problems and Solutions, 1938–1964.* [4.4]

Greitzer, Samuel L. *International Mathematical Olympiads, 1959–1977.* [4.4]

* Gries, David. *The Science of Programming.* [22.12]

* Grinstein, Louise S. *Women of Mathematics: A Bio-bibliographic Sourcebook.* [5.10]

* ——. *Calculus: Readings from the Mathematics Teacher.* [6.5]

** ——. *Mathematics Education in Secondary Schools and Two-Year Colleges: A Sourcebook.* [5.8]

Grob, Bernard. *Mathematics for Basic Electronics.* [16.5]

** Gross, Donald. *Fundamentals of Queueing Theory.* [19.5]

Gross, Maurice. *Mathematical Models in Linguistics.* [25.1]

Grossman, Stanley I. *Algebra and Trigonometry.* [6.2]

——. *Calculus.* [6.3]

* Grouws, Douglas A. *Perspectives on Research on Effective Mathematics Teaching.* [5.12]

** Grünbaum, Branko. *Tilings and Patterns.* [14.5]

* Guest, Russell J. *Mathematics for Plumbers and Pipe Fitters.* [16.2]

Guillen, Michael. *Bridges to Infinity: The Human Side of Mathematics.* [1.2]

** Guy, Richard K. *Unsolved Problems in Number Theory.* [11.3]

——. *Winning Ways for Your Mathematical Plays.* [4.1]

H

* Haberman, Richard. *Mathematical Models, Mechanical Vibrations, Population Dynamics, and Traffic Flow: An Introduction to Applied Mathematics.* [19.2]

Hacking, Ian. *The Emergence of Probability.* [3.10]

** Hadlock, Charles R. *Field Theory and Its Classical Problems.* [13.5]

Haggard, Gary M. *Applied Mathematics for Business, Economics, and the Social Sciences.* [17.2]

——. *Calculus and Its Applications.* [17.4]

Haines, Robert G. *Math Principles for Food Service Occupations.* [16.2]

Hald, Anders. *A History of Probability and Statistics and Their Applications Before 1750.* [3.10]

Hall, A. Rupert. *Philosophers at War: The Quarrel Between Newton and Leibniz.* [3.8]

** Hall, Marshall, Jr. *The Theory of Groups.* [13.3]

* Hallam, Thomas G. *Mathematical Ecology: An Introduction.* [23.2]

* Halmos, Paul R. *Finite-Dimensional Vector Spaces.* [12.2]

——. *I Have A Photographic Memory.* [3.6]

* ——. *I Want To Be A Mathematician: An Automathography in Three Parts.* [3.2]

——. *Lectures on Boolean Algebras.* [13.2]

*** ——. *Naive Set Theory.* [9.3]

Halsted, George B. *Girolamo Saccheri's Euclides Vindicatus.* [3.4]

* Hamilton, L.F. *Calculations of Analytic Chemistry.* [16.6]

Hamming, Richard W. *Methods of Mathematics Applied to Calculus, Probability, and Statistics.* [6.3]

Hanan, James. *Lindenmayer Systems, Fractals, and Plants.* [23.2]

Hansen, Viggo P. *Computers in Mathematics Education: 1984 Yearbook.* [5.14]

Harary, Frank. *Distance in Graphs.* [10.4]

——. *Graph Theory.* [10.4]

* Hardy, G.H. *Introduction to the Theory of Numbers.* [11.3]

——. *Inequalities.* [8.6]

*** ——. *A Mathematician's Apology.* [1.2]

* ——. *Ramanujan.* [3.2]

* Harel, David. *Algorithmics: The Spirit of Computing.* [22.1]

Harper, John R. *Lectures on Algebraic Topology.* [15.3]

** Harris, Carl M. *Fundamentals of Queueing Theory.* [19.5]

Hart, Sergiu. *Handbook of Game Theory with Applications to Economics.* [19.3]

* Hart, Therese A. *A Challenge of Numbers: People in the Mathematical Sciences.* [5.1]

Hart, W.L. *Mathematics of Investment.* [17.5]

*** Hayden, Jerome D. *Fundamental Mathematics for Health Careers.* [16.3]

* Hearn, Donald. *Computer Graphics.* [22.14]

Heath, Thomas L. *The Works of Archimedes.* [3.4]

** ——. *A History of Greek Mathematics.* [3.5]

——. *Apollonius of Perga.* [3.4]

——. *Aristarchus of Samos: The Ancient Copernicus.* [3.4]

——. *Diophantus of Alexandria.* [3.4]

** ——. *The Thirteen Books of Euclid's Elements.* [3.4]

Hecht, G.W. *Calculus for Electronics.* [16.5]

Heeren, Vern E. *Mathematical Ideas.* [1.4]

Heinz, Kunle. *Proceedings of the Third International Congress on Mathematical Education.* [5.6]

* Hendrix, T.G. *Mathematics for Auto Mechanics.* [16.2]
* Henkin, Leon. *Mathematics: Report of the Project 2061 Phase I Mathematics Panel.* [5.6]
* Henle, Michael. *A Combinatorial Introduction to Topology.* [15.3]

Henry, Loren L. *Activities for Junior High School and Middle School Mathematics.* [5.8]
* Herman, Stephen L. *Practical Problems in Mathematics for Electricians.* [16.2]
* Hersh, Reuben. *Descartes' Dream: The World According to Mathematics.* [1.2]
* ———. *The Mathematical Experience.* [1.2]

Herstein, I.N. *Matters Mathematical.* [1.4]
** ———. *Abstract Algebra.* [13.1]
* ———. *Topics in Algebra.* [13.2]

Hewitt, Edwin. *Real and Abstract Analysis: A Modern Treatment of the Theory of Functions of a Real Variable.* [8.2]

Heyman, D.P. *Handbook in Operations Research and Management Science.* [19.5]

Hiebert, James. *Number Concepts and Operations in the Middle Grades.* [5.12]

Higgins, John C. *Mathematics: People, Problems, Results.* [1.1]

Highers, Michael P. *Mathematics for the Allied Health Professions.* [16.3]
** Hilbert, David. *Geometry and the Imagination.* [14.1]
* ———. *Methods of Mathematical Physics.* [24.3]
* Hildebrandt, Stefan. *Mathematics and Optimal Form.* [14.1]

Hill, David R. *Experiments in Computational Matrix Algebra.* [18.3]
* Hill, Raymond. *A First Course in Coding Theory.* [10.5]
*** Hillier, Frederick S. *Introduction to Operations Research.* [19.1]
* Hillman, Abraham P. *A First Undergraduate Course in Abstract Algebra.* [13.1]
* Hilton, Peter J. *Build Your Own Polyhedra.* [14.5]

Hirsch, Christian R. *The Secondary School Mathematics Curriculum: 1985 Yearbook.* [5.8]
* Hirsch, Morris W. *Differential Equations, Dynamical Systems, and Linear Algebra.* [7.2]
* Hirshfield, Stuart. *The Analytical Engine.* [22.1]

Hirst, Ann. *Proceedings of the Sixth International Congress on Mathematical Education.* [5.6]

Hirst, Keith. *Proceedings of the Sixth International Congress on Mathematical Education.* [5.6]
* Hoaglin, David C. *Understanding Robust and Exploratory Data Analysis.* [21.5]
———. *Applications, Basics, and Computing of Exploratory Data Analysis.* [21.5]

Hoare, C.A.R. *Structured Programming.* [22.6]

Hobbs, Margie. *Introduction to Technical Mathematics.* [16.1]
** Hodges, Andrew. *Alan Turing, The Enigma.* [3.2]

Hodges, Joseph L. *Elements of Finite Probability.* [20.2]

Hodges, W. *Building Models by Games.* [9.4]

Hodson, F.R. *Mathematics and Computers in Archaeology.* [25.1]

Hoenig, Alan. *Applied Finite Mathematics.* [10.2]

Hoffer, Alan. *Geometry.* [14.3]

Hoffman, Edward G. *Practical Problems in Mathematics for Machinists.* [16.2]
* Hoffman, Kenneth. *Linear Algebra.* [12.2]

Hoffman, Paul. *Archimedes' Revenge: The Joys and Perils of Mathematics.* [1.2]
* Hoffmann, Banesh. *Albert Einstein: Creator and Rebel.* [3.2]

Hoffmann, Laurence D. *Calculus for Business, Economics, and the Social and Life Sciences.* [17.4]
* Hofstadter, Douglas R. *Gödel, Escher, Bach: An Eternal Golden Braid.* [1.2]
———. *Metamagical Themas: Questing for the Essence of Mind and Pattern.* [1.2]

Hogg, Robert V. *Introduction to Mathematical Statistics.* [21.4]
———. *Loss Distributions.* [17.7]
———. *Engineering Statistics.* [21.4]
* ———. *Probability and Statistical Inference.* [21.4]
———. *Studies in Statistics.* [21.1]

Hohn, Franz E. *Applied Modern Algebra.* [13.1]
** Hoit, Laura K. *The Arithmetic of Dosages and Solutions.* [16.3]

Holden, Alan. *Orderly Tangles: Cloverleafs, Gordian Knots, and Regular Polylinks.* [14.5]

Hollander, Myles. *The Statistical Exorcist: Dispelling Statistics Anxiety.* [21.1]

Hollingdale, Stuart. *Makers of Mathematics.* [3.1]
* Honsberger, Ross. *Ingenuity in Mathematics.* [1.2]
* ———. *Mathematical Gems.* [1.2]
* ———. *Mathematical Morsels.* [1.2]
* ———. *Mathematical Plums.* [1.2]
* ———. *More Mathematical Morsels.* [1.2]
*** Hopcroft, John E. *Data Structures and Algorithms.* [22.4]
** ———. *The Design and Analysis of Computer Algorithms.* [22.8]
** ———. *Introduction to Automata Theory, Languages, and Computation.* [22.15]
** Hoppensteadt, Frank C. *Mathematical Methods of Population Biology.* [23.5]
———. *Mathematical Theories of Populations: Demographics, Genetics, and Epidemics.* [23.5]
* Hordern, Edward. *Sliding Piece Puzzles.* [4.2]
* Horn, Paul. *LISP.* [22.7]

Hornsby, E. John, Jr. *Mathematical Ideas.* [1.4]

Horowitz, Ellis. *Fundamentals of Data Structures in Pascal.* [22.4]
** ———. *Programming Languages: A Grand Tour.* [22.6]

Hosack, John M. *Calculus: An Integrated Approach.* [6.3]
———. *Explorations in Calculus with a Computer Algebra System.* [6.3]

Hossack, I.B. *Introductory Statistics with Applications in General Insurance.* [17.3]
* Houde, Richard. *How to Use Conjecturing and Microcomputers to Teach Geometry.* [5.14]

Howland, Joseph W. *Nursing Simplified: Math Logic.* [16.3]

Howson, A. Geoffrey. *The Influence of Computers and Informatics on Mathematics and Its Teaching.* [5.14]

———. *The Popularization of Mathematics.* [5.1]

———. *Developments in Mathematical Education: Proceedings of the Second International Congress on Mathematical Education.* [5.6]

———. *Curriculum Development in Mathematics.* [5.6]

———. *A Handbook of Terms Used in Algebra and Analysis.* [2.1]

Hoyle, Fred. *From Stonehenge to Modern Cosmology.* [24.5]

Hubbard, John H. *Differential Equations: A Dynamical Systems Approach.* [7.1]

Huff, Darrell. *How to Lie with Statistics.* [21.1]

———. *How to Take a Chance.* [20.1]

Hungerford, Thomas W. *Abstract Algebra: An Introduction.* [13.1]

* Hunter, J. Stuart. *Statistics for Experimenters: An Introduction to Design, Data Analysis, and Model Building.* [21.4]

* Hunter, William G. *Statistics for Experimenters: An Introduction to Design, Data Analysis, and Model Building.* [21.4]

* Huntley, H.E. *The Divine Proportion: A Study in Mathematical Beauty.* [1.6]

Hustead, E.C. *100 Years of Mortality.* [17.7]

Huth, H. *Practical Problems in Mathematics for Carpenters.* [16.2]

I

Impagliazzo, J. *Deterministic Aspects of Mathematical Demography.* [23.5]

* Infeld, Leopold. *Whom the Gods Love: The Story of Evariste Galois.* [3.2]

Ingrao, Bruna. *The Invisible Hand: Economic Equilibrium in the History of Science.* [25.2]

Inhelder, B. *The Child's Conception of Geometry.* [5.3]

* Iooss, Gérard. *Elementary Stability and Bifurcation Theory.* [7.2]

** Isenberg, Cyril. *The Science of Soap Films and Soap Bubbles.* [24.1]

** Isern, Margarita. *Technical Mathematics.* [16.1]

Israel, Giorgio. *The Invisible Hand: Economic Equilibrium in the History of Science.* [25.2]

Iverson, Gudmund R. *Bayesian Statistical Inference.* [21.8]

* Iyanaga, Shôkichi. *Encyclopedic Dictionary of Mathematics.* [2.3]

J

Jackson, Brad. *Applied Combinatorics with Problem Solving.* [10.3]

* Jacobs, Harold R. *Geometry.* [14.3]

* ———. *Mathematics: A Human Endeavor.* [1.4]

* Jaffe, A.J. *Misused Statistics: Straight Talk for Twisted Numbers.* [21.1]

** James, Glenn. *Mathematical Dictionary.* [2.1]

** James, Robert C. *Mathematical Dictionary.* [2.1]

Janusz, Gerald J. *Introduction to Modern Algebra.* [13.1]

Jeffreys, Bertha S. *Methods of Mathematical Physics.* [24.3]

Jeffreys, Sir Harold. *Methods of Mathematical Physics.* [24.3]

John, Fritz. *Introduction to Calculus and Analysis.* [6.4]

———. *Partial Differential Equations.* [7.2]

* Johnson, David S. *Computers and Intractability: A Guide to the Theory of NP-Completeness.* [22.9]

Johnson, John. *Prof. E. McSquared's Expanded Intergalactic Version: A Calculus Primer.* [6.5]

** Johnson, Norman L. *Encyclopedia of Statistical Sciences.* [2.3]

Johnson, R.H. *Quantitative Methods for Management.* [17.6]

Johnson, Richard A. *Applied Multivariate Statistical Analysis.* [21.8]

Johnsonbaugh, Richard. *Discrete Mathematics.* [10.1]

Jolley, L.B.W. *Summation of Series.* [2.2]

* Jones, Douglas. *Perspectives on Research on Effective Mathematics Teaching.* [5.12]

Jones, D.S. *Elementary Information Theory.* [24.6]

Jones, Phillip S. *A History of Mathematics Education in the United States and Canada: 32nd Yearbook.* [5.5]

Jordan, C.W. *Life Contingencies.* [17.7]

* Joseph, Daniel D. *Elementary Stability and Bifurcation Theory.* [7.2]

K

Kac, Mark. *Discrete Thoughts: Essays on Mathematics, Science, and Philosophy.* [1.3]

* ———. *Statistical Independence in Probability, Analysis, and Number Theory.* [20.3]

Kadane, Joseph B. *Statistics and the Law.* [21.1]

Kahane, J.-P. *The Influence of Computers and Informatics on Mathematics and Its Teaching.* [5.14]

———. *The Popularization of Mathematics.* [5.1]

Kahneman, Daniel. *Judgment Under Uncertainty: Heuristics and Biases.* [20.1]

Kainen, Paul C. *The Four-Color Problem: Assaults and Conquest.* [10.4]

*** Kanigel, Robert. *The Man Who Knew Infinity: A Life of the Indian Genius Ramanujan.* [3.2]

Kao, T.I. *Was Pythagoras Chinese? An Examination of Right Triangle Theory in Ancient China.* [3.5]

Kaplansky, Irving. *Commutative Rings.* [13.6]

———. *Fields and Rings.* [13.4]

———. *Matters Mathematical.* [1.4]

** Kappraff, Jay. *Connections: The Geometric Bridge Between Art and Science.* [1.2]

Karlin, Samuel. *An Introduction to Stochastic Modeling.* [20.4]

Kaufmann, Jerome E. *College Algebra and Trigonometry.* [6.2]

* Kawada, Yukiyosi. *Encyclopedic Dictionary of Mathematics.* [2.3]

Kazarinoff, Nicholas D. *Analytic Inequalities.* [8.6]

Kee, Joyce L. *Clinical Calculations with Applications to General and Specialty Areas.* [16.3]

Keedwell, A.D. *Latin Squares and Their Applications.* [10.3]

* Keen, Linda. *Chaos and Fractals: The Mathematics Behind the Computer Graphics.* [8.3]

Keisler, H. Jerome. *Elementary Calculus.* [6.3]
————. *Model Theory.* [9.4]

Keitel, Christine. *Curriculum Development in Mathematics.* [5.6]

* Keith, Sandra. *Winning Women Into Mathematics.* [5.10]

Kelley, John L. *General Topology.* [15.1]

** Kellison, Stephen G. *The Theory of Interest.* [17.5]

* Kelly, L.M. *The William Lowell Putnam Mathematical Competition: Problems and Solutions, 1938–1964.* [4.4]

Kemeny, John G. *Finite Markov Chains.* [20.4]
————. *Mathematical Models in the Social Sciences.* [25.1]

** ————. *Introduction to Finite Mathematics.* [10.2]
————. *Man and the Computer.* [22.2]

Kempe, A.B. *How to Draw a Straight Line.* [14.3]

* Kenschaft, Patricia C. *Winning Women Into Mathematics.* [5.10]

Kernighan, Brian W. *The UNIX Programming Environment.* [22.10]

*** ————. *The Elements of Programming Style.* [22.6]

* ————. *The C Programming Language.* [22.7]

*** Keyfitz, Nathan. *Demography Through Problems.* [23.5]

** ————. *Mathematical Demography.* [23.5]

Khinchin, A. Ya. *An Elementary Introduction to the Theory of Probability.* [20.2]
————. *Three Pearls of Number Theory.* [11.2]

Khoury, Sarkis J. *Mathematical Methods in Finance and Economics.* [25.2]

Kidder, Tracy. *The Soul of a New Machine.* [22.1]

* Kieran, Carolyn. *Research Issues in the Learning and Teaching of Algebra.* [5.12]

Kilgour, D. Marc. *Game Theory and National Security.* [19.3]

* Kilpatrick, Jeremy. *Thinking Through Mathematics: Fostering Inquiry and Communication in Mathematics Classrooms.* [5.6]
————. *Mathematics and Cognition.* [5.3]
————. *Academic Preparation in Mathematics: Teaching for Transition From High School to College.* [5.1]
————. *Curriculum Development in Mathematics.* [5.6]

* Kimura, Moto. *An Introduction to Population Genetics Theory.* [23.4]

** Kincaid, David R. *Numerical Analysis: Mathematics of Scientific Computing.* [18.1]

————. *Numerical Mathematics and Computing.* [18.1]

King, G. Brooks. *Problems for General Chemistry and Qualitative Analysis.* [16.6]

Kingsland, Sharon E. *Modeling Nature: Episodes in the History of Population Ecology.* [23.2]

** Klamkin, Murray S. *1001 Problems in High School Mathematics.* [4.4]
————. *International Mathematical Olympiads, 1978–1985 and Forty Supplementary Problems.* [4.4]

* ————. *Mathematical Modelling: Classroom Notes in Applied Mathematics.* [19.2]

Klarner, David A. *The Mathematical Gardner.* [4.6]

* Klaus, Berthold. *LISP.* [22.7]

Kleene, Stephen C. *Introduction to Metamathematics.* [9.2]

* ————. *Mathematical Logic.* [9.2]

Klein, Jacob. *Greek Mathematical Thought and the Origin of Algebra.* [3.5]

* Kline, Morris. *Calculus: An Intuitive and Physical Approach.* [6.3]
————. *Mathematical Thought from Ancient to Modern Times.* [3.1]
————. *Mathematics and the Search for Knowledge.* [1.2]
————. *Mathematics in Western Culture.* [3.1]
————. *Mathematics: The Loss of Certainty.* [1.2]

Klopfer, L.E. *Toward the Thinking Curriculum: Current Cognitive Research.* [5.12]

Klosinski, Leonard F. *The William Lowell Putnam Mathematical Competition: Problems and Solutions, 1965–1984.* [4.4]

Klugman, S. *Loss Distributions.* [17.7]

Kneebone, G.T. *Mathematical Logic and the Foundations of Mathematics.* [9.2]

Knight, Raymond M. *Technical Mathematics with Calculus.* [16.7]

Knopp, Konrad. *Infinite Sequences and Series.* [6.4]
————. *Theory and Application of Infinite Series.* [6.4]
————. *Theory of Functions.* [8.4]

Knörrer, Horst. *Plane Algebraic Curves.* [14.7]

** Knuth, Donald E. *Concrete Mathematics: A Foundation for Computer Science.* [10.3]
————. *Mathematical Writing.* [5.9]
————. *Surreal Numbers.* [1.5]

*** ————. *The Art of Computer Programming.* [22.8]
————. *The TEX Book.* [22.15]

Koblitz, Ann Hibner. *A Convergence of Lives, Sofia Kovalevskaia: Scientist, Writer, Revolutionary.* [3.2]

Koehler, Vera J. *Programmed Mathematics of Drugs and Solutions.* [16.3]

Koffman, Elliot B. *Pascal: Problem Solving and Program Design.* [22.7]

Kolatis, Maria S. *Mathematics for Data Processing and Computing.* [16.4]

Kolman, Bernard. *Elementary Linear Programming with Applications.* [19.4]

* ————. *Applied Finite Mathematics.* [10.2]

Kolmogorov, Andrei N. *Introductory Real Analysis.* [8.2]

** ———. *Mathematics: Its Content, Methods, and Meaning.* [1.1]

* ———. *Foundations of the Theory of Probability.* [20.5]

** Koopmans, Lambert H. *Introduction to Contemporary Statistical Methods.* [21.2]

Kordemsky, Boris A. *The Moscow Puzzles: 359 Mathematical Recreations.* [4.3]

Korsh, James F. *Data Structures, Algorithms, and Program Style Using C.* [22.4]

Korth, Henry F. *Database System Concepts.* [22.5]

** Kotz, Samuel. *Encyclopedia of Statistical Sciences.* [2.3]

*** Kraitchik, Maurice. *Mathematical Recreations.* [4.1]

** Kramer, Arthur D. *Fundamentals of Technical Mathematics with Calculus.* [16.7]

** Kramer, Edna E. *The Nature and Growth of Modern Mathematics.* [3.1]

* Krantz, Steven G. *Complex Analysis: The Geometric Viewpoint.* [8.4]

** Krause, Eugene F. *Taxicab Geometry: An Adventure in Non-Euclidean Geometry.* [14.1]

Kreyszig, Erwin. *Advanced Engineering Mathematics.* [24.2]

* Kruse, Robert L. *Data Structures and Program Design.* [22.4]

* Kuhfittig, Peter K.F. *Basic Technical Mathematics with Calculus.* [16.7]

——— . *Introduction to Technical Mathematics.* [16.1]

Kulm, Gerald. *Assessing Higher Order Thinking in Mathematics.* [5.13]

Kumpel, P.G. *Linear Algebra with Applications to Differential Equations.* [12.1]

* Kunze, Ray. *Linear Algebra.* [12.2]

L

** Lakatos, Imre. *Proofs and Refutations: The Logic of Mathematical Discovery.* [9.2]

Lam, Lay Yong. *A Critical Study of the Yang Hui Suan Fa: A Thirteenth-century Chinese Mathematical Treatise.* [3.4]

Landau, Edmund G.H. *The Foundations of Analysis.* [8.1]

** Landwehr, James M. *Exploring Data.* [21.1]

** ———. *Exploring Surveys and Information From Samples.* [21.1]

Lane, Melissa J. *Women and Minorities in Science and Engineering.* [5.10]

Lang, Serge. *Algebra.* [13.2]

* ———. *Introduction to Linear Algebra.* [12.1]

——— . *Linear Algebra.* [12.2]

** ———. *The Beauty of Doing Mathematics: Three Public Dialogues.* [1.6]

Lange, W.H. *Mathematics for Business and New Consumers.* [17.1]

LaPointe, Archie. *A World of Differences: An International Assessment of Mathematics and Science.* [5.13]

Larrabee, Tracy. *Mathematical Writing.* [5.9]

Larsen, M.D. *Calculus with Applications.* [17.4]

* Larsen, Richard J. *Statistics in the Real World: A Book of Examples.* [21.3]

Larson, Loren C. *The William Lowell Putnam Mathematical Competition: Problems and Solutions, 1965–1984.* [4.4]

——— . *Algebra and Trigonometry Refresher for Calculus Students.* [6.2]

** ———. *Problem-Solving Through Problems.* [4.4]

* Latham, Marcia L. *The Geometry of René Descartes.* [3.4]

Latta, Gordon. *Complex Variables.* [8.4]

* Lauwerier, Hans. *Fractals: Endlessly Repeated Geometrical Figures.* [8.3]

** Lavrent'ev, M.A. *Mathematics: Its Content, Methods, and Meaning.* [1.1]

* Lawler, Eugene L. *The Traveling Salesman Problem: A Guided Tour of Combinatorial Optimization.* [19.5]

Lawrence, J. Dennis. *A Catalog of Special Plane Curves.* [2.2]

* Lay, David C. *Calculus and Its Applications.* [6.3]

Lazarsfeld, Paul F. *Mathematical Thinking in the Social Sciences.* [25.1]

LeBlanc, Richard J., Jr. *Crafting a Compiler.* [22.13]

** Leder, Gilah. *Mathematics and Gender.* [5.10]

Ledermann, Walter. *Analysis.* [24.1]

Ledolter, Johannes. *Engineering Statistics.* [21.4]

Lee, Shin-Ying. *Mathematical Knowledge of Japanese, Chinese, and American Elementary School Children.* [5.13]

* LeFevor, C.S. *Mathematics for Auto Mechanics.* [16.2]

Leffin, Walter W. *Introduction to Technical Mathematics.* [16.1]

Lehmann, E.L. *Nonparametrics: Statistical Methods Based on Ranks.* [21.8]

——— . *Elements of Finite Probability.* [20.2]

* Leinbach, L. Carl. *The Laboratory Approach to Teaching Calculus.* [5.9]

* Leithold, Louis. *Before Calculus: Functions, Graphs, and Analytic Geometry.* [6.2]

*** Leitzel, James R.C. *A Call For Change: Recommendations for the Mathematical Preparation of Teachers of Mathematics.* [5.9]

Leitzel, Joan R. *Transition to College Mathematics.* [6.2]

Lerner, Norbert. *Algebra and Trigonometry: A Pre-Calculus Approach.* [6.2]

Lester, Frank. *How To Evaluate Progress in Problem Solving.* [5.11]

Levasseur, Kenneth. *Applied Discrete Structures for Computer Science.* [10.1]

LeVeque, William J. *Topics in Number Theory.* [11.3]

Levi, Howard. *Polynomials, Power Series, and Calculus.* [6.3]

* Levin, Simon A. *Mathematical Ecology: An Introduction.* [23.2]

* ———. *Studies in Mathematical Biology.* [23.1]

** Levinson, Norman. *Theory of Ordinary Differential Equations.* [7.2]

Levy, David N.L. *Computer Games I.* [22.11]

* Lewis, Philip G. *Approaching Precalculus Mathematics Discretely: Explorations in a Computer Environment.* [6.2]

Lǐ Yǎn. *Chinese Mathematics: A Concise History.* [3.5]

Libeskind, S. *Logo.* [14.6]

** Lieber, Lillian R. *Galois and the Theory of Groups: A Bright Star in Mathesis.* [13.5]

*** Lieberman, Gerald J. *Introduction to Operations Research.* [19.1]

Lin, C.C. *Mathematics Applied to Deterministic Problems in the Natural Sciences.* [24.3]

** Lindgren, Harry. *Geometric Dissections.* [4.6]

Lindgren, Michael. *Glory and Failure.* [3.11]

* Lindquist, Mary M. *Learning and Teaching Geometry, K–12: 1987 Yearbook.* [5.6]

———. *Results from the Fourth Mathematics Assessment of the National Assessment of Educational Progress.* [5.13]

Lines, Malcolm. *Think of a Number.* [4.2]

Lipschutz, Seymour. *Schaum's Solved Problems Series: 3000 Solved Problems in Linear Algebra.* [12.1]

Littlewood, J.E. *Inequalities.* [8.6]

Liusternik, L. *Elements of Functional Analysis.* [8.5]

Lloyd, E. Keith. *Graph Theory, 1736–1936.* [10.4]

Lockwood, E.H. *Geometric Symmetry.* [14.5]

———. *A Book of Curves.* [14.8]

Logothetis, N. *Probability Distributions.* [20.3]

Loomis, E. *The Pythagorean Proposition.* [14.3]

Lotka, A.J. *Elements of Mathematical Biology.* [23.1]

Lott, Johnny W. *Logo.* [14.6]

* Loyd, Sam. *Sam Loyd's Cyclopedia of 5000 Puzzles, Tricks, and Conundrums.* [4.3]

** Lucas, William F. *Political and Related Models.* [25.3]

———. *Game Theory and its Applications.* [19.3]

* ———. *Discrete and System Models.* [19.2]

** Luce, Robert Duncan. *Games and Decisions.* [19.3]

Lyng, M.J. *Applied Technical Mathematics.* [16.1]

Lyusternik, L.A. *The Shortest Lines: Variational Problems.* [14.8]

M

* MacDonald, I.G. *Introduction to Commutative Algebra.* [13.6]

MacGillavry, Caroline H. *Fantasy & Symmetry: The Periodic Drawings of M.S. Escher.* [14.5]

* MacHale, Desmond. *George Boole: His Life and Work.* [3.2]

Machover, Moshé. *A Course in Mathematical Logic.* [9.2]

* Mackey, M.C. *From Clocks to Chaos: The Rhythms of Life.* [23.6]

Mac Lane, Saunders. *Algebra.* [13.2]

*** ———. *A Survey of Modern Algebra.* [13.1]

———. *Mathematics, Form and Function.* [9.1]

MacLennan, Bruce J. *Principles of Programming Languages: Design, Evaluation, and Implementation.* [22.6]

Macmillan, R.H. *Geometric Symmetry.* [14.5]

* Madison, Bernard L. *A Challenge of Numbers: People in the Mathematical Sciences.* [5.1]

Maistrov, Leonid E. *Probability Theory: A Historical Sketch.* [3.10]

* Maki, Daniel P. *Finite Mathematics.* [10.2]

———. *Mathematical Models and Applications with Emphasis on the Social, Life, and Management Sciences.* [25.1]

Malkevitch, Joseph. *Graphs, Models, and Finite Mathematics.* [10.2]

* Manber, Udi. *Introduction to Algorithms: A Creative Approach.* [22.8]

* Mandelbrot, Benoit. *The Fractal Geometry of Nature.* [8.3]

Mangel, Marc. *Dynamic Modeling in Behavioral Ecology.* [23.2]

** Marcus-Roberts, Helen. *Life Science Models.* [23.1]

Margolis, Emil J. *Chemical Principles in Calculations of Tonic Equilibria.* [16.6]

** Marsden, Jerrold E. *Calculus III.* [6.4]

** ———. *Calculus.* [6.3]

Marshal, Sally M. *Clinical Calculations with Applications to General and Specialty Areas.* [16.3]

* Martin, Edward. *Elements of Mathematics, Book B: Problem Book.* [6.1]

Mason, John H. *Thinking Mathematically.* [5.11]

———. *Learning and Doing Mathematics.* [5.11]

Mason, R.D. *Mathematics for Business and New Consumers.* [17.1]

* Massey, William S. *Algebraic Topology: An Introduction.* [15.3]

** Mathematical Sciences Education Board. *Reshaping School Mathematics: A Philosophy and Framework for Curriculum.* [5.1]

Mathews, John H. *Numerical Methods for Computer Science, Engineering, and Mathematics.* [18.1]

* Matlock, Bill J. *Practical Problems in Mathematics for Welders.* [16.2]

* Maurer, Stephen B. *Discrete Algorithmic Mathematics.* [10.1]

May, Donald C., Jr. *Handbook of Probability and Statistics with Tables.* [2.2]

May, Kenneth O. *Lectures on Calculus.* [6.5]

———. *Bibliography and Research Manual of the History of Mathematics.* [2.4]

———. *Index of the American Mathematical Monthly, Volumes 1–80 (1894–1973).* [2.5]

* Mazumdar, J. *An Introduction to Mathematical Physiology and Biology.* [23.6]

Mbili, L.S.R. *Mathematical Challenge! One Hundred Problems for the Olympiad Enthusiast.* [4.4]

* McCabe, George P. *Introduction to the Practice of Statistics.* [21.2]

McClave, James T. *Statistics.* [21.2]

———. *A Second Course in Business Statistics: Regression Analysis.* [17.3]

McCleary, John. *The History of Modern Mathematics.* [3.1]

McCoy, Neal H. *Introduction to Modern Algebra.* [13.1]

———. *Rings and Ideals.* [13.4]

———. *The Theory of Rings.* [13.4]

McCullough, Robert N. *Mathematics for Data Processing.* [16.4]

McCutcheon, J.J. *An Introduction to the Mathematics of Finance.* [17.5]

McDonald, John. *The Game of Business.* [19.3]

* McDonald, T.M. *Mathematical Models for Social and Management Scientists.* [17.6]

McGettrick, Andrew D. *Graded Problems in Computer Science.* [22.3]

* McHale, Thomas J. *Technical Mathematics I and II.* [16.1]

McKnight, Curtis C. *The Underachieving Curriculum: Assessing U.S. School Mathematics From An International Perspective.* [5.13]

McLeod, Douglas. *Affect and Mathematical Problem Solving: A New Perspective.* [5.11]

McLone, R.R. *Mathematical Modelling.* [19.2]

McMackin, Frank J. *Mathematics of the Shop.* [16.2]

Mead, Nancy. *A World of Differences: An International Assessment of Mathematics and Science.* [5.13]

Mehlhorn, Kurt. *Data Structures and Algorithms.* [22.4]

Mellin-Olsen, Steig. *The Politics of Mathematics Education: Mathematics Education Library.* [5.2]

* Mellish, C.S. *Programming in Prolog.* [22.7]

Melzak, Z.A. *Mathematical Ideas, Modeling, and Applications.* [19.2]

* Mendelson, Elliott. *Introduction to Mathematical Logic.* [9.2]

———. *Schaum's 3000 Solved Problems in Calculus.* [6.5]

Mendenhall, William. *A Second Course in Business Statistics: Regression Analysis.* [17.3]

* ———. *Elementary Survey Sampling.* [21.7]

———. *Mathematical Statistics with Applications.* [21.4]

* Menninger, Karl. *Number Words and Number Symbols: A Cultural History of Numbers.* [3.7]

* Merzbach, Uta C. *A Century of Mathematics in America.* [3.6]

*** ———. *A History of Mathematics.* [3.1]

Messick, David M. *Mathematical Thinking in Behavioral Sciences.* [25.4]

Mestre, Jose P. *Linguistic and Cultural Influences on Learning Mathematics.* [5.4]

* Meyer, Bertrand. *Introduction to the Theory of Programming Languages.* [22.6]

Meyer, Walter J. *Concepts of Mathematical Modeling.* [19.2]

———. *Graphs, Models, and Finite Mathematics.* [10.2]

* Michaels, Brenda. *Calculus: Readings from the Mathematics Teacher.* [6.5]

Michels, Leo. *Mathematics for Health Sciences.* [16.3]

* Mickens, Ronald E. *Difference Equations.* [10.5]

* Midici, Geraldine Ann. *Drug Dosage Calculations: A Guide to Clinical Calculation.* [16.3]

Miertschin, S.L. *Technical Mathematics with Calculus.* [16.7]

Miller, Charles D. *Mathematical Ideas.* [1.4]

Miller, Nancy E. *File Structures Using Pascal.* [22.4]

Miller, Richard K. *Ordinary Differential Equations.* [7.1]

Miller, Robert B. *Intermediate Business Statistics.* [17.3]

Milnor, John W. *Topology from the Differentiable Viewpoint.* [15.4]

Minsky, Marvin. *Perceptrons: An Introduction to Computational Geometry.* [22.11]

Misner, Charles W. *Gravitation.* [24.4]

Mizrahi, Abe. *Finite Mathematics with Applications for Business and Social Sciences.* [17.2]

Mohamed, J.L. *Numerical Algorithms.* [18.5]

Moise, Edwin E. *Geometry.* [14.3]

Moler, Cleve B. *Experiments in Computational Matrix Algebra.* [18.3]

*** Montgomery, Hugh L. *An Introduction to the Theory of Numbers.* [11.1]

Moore, Claude S. *Applied Math for Technicians.* [16.1]

* Moore, David S. *Introduction to the Practice of Statistics.* [21.2]

*** ———. *Statistics: Concepts and Controversies.* [21.2]

* Moore, George. *Practical Problems in Mathematics for Automotive Technicians.* [16.2]

Moore, Susan G. *Nursing Simplified: Math Logic.* [16.3]

Moorhead, E.J. *Our Yesterdays: The History of the Actuarial Profession in North America, 1805–1979.* [17.7]

Moreau, R. *The Computer Comes of Age: The People, the Hardware, and the Software.* [22.1]

Morrel, Bernard B. *Applied Calculus.* [17.4]

Morrey, C.B. *A First Course in Real Analysis.* [8.2]

** Morrison, Philip. *Powers of Ten.* [1.2]

** Morrison, Phylis. *Powers of Ten.* [1.2]

Moscardini, A.O. *Learning the Art of Mathematical Modelling.* [19.2]

** Moser, William. *1001 Problems in High School Mathematics.* [4.4]

* Moses, Lincoln E. *Think and Explain with Statistics.* [21.3]

* Mosteller, Frederick. *Understanding Robust and Exploratory Data Analysis.* [21.5]

** ———. *Data Analysis and Regression: A Second Course in Statistics.* [21.6]

** ———. *Medical Uses of Statistics.* [23.6]

*** ———. *Statistics: A Guide to the Unknown.* [21.1]

———. *Beginning Statistics with Data Analysis.* [21.5]

———. *Probability with Statistical Applications.* [20.2]

* ———. *Fifty Challenging Problems in Probability with Solutions.* [20.1]

Mrachek, Leonard A. *Practical Mathematics.* [16.2]

Munkres, James R. *Topology: A First Course.* [15.1]

Murphy, Dennis. *Merchandising Mathematics.* [16.2]

* Murray, J.D. *Mathematical Biology.* [23.1]

** Murty, U.S.R. *Graph Theory with Applications.* [10.4]

N

** Nagel, Ernest. *Gödel's Proof.* [9.2]
 * Nagell, Trygve. *Introduction to Number Theory.* [11.1]
   Nagy, Bela Sz. *Functional Analysis.* [8.5]
** National Council of Teachers of Mathematics. *A Sourcebook of Applications of School Mathematics.* [5.6]
   ———. *Cumulative Index, The Arithmetic Teacher: 1974-1983.* [2.5]
*** ———. *Curriculum and Evaluation Standards for School Mathematics.* [5.6]
*** ———. *Professional Standards for Teaching Mathematics.* [5.6]
 * ———. *The Mathematics Teacher: Cumulative Indices.* [2.5]
*** National Research Council. *Everybody Counts: A Report to the Nation on the Future of Mathematics Education.* [5.1]
*** ———. *Moving Beyond Myths: Revitalizing Undergraduate Mathematics.* [5.1]
   ———. *Renewing U.S. Mathematics: A Plan for the 1990s.* [5.1]
   ———. *Renewing U.S. Mathematics: Critical Resource for the Future.* [5.1]
*** Nelson, C. Robert. *Elementary Technical Mathematics.* [16.1]
 * Nelson, R.D. *The Penguin Dictionary of Mathematics.* [2.1]
 * Nemhauser, George L. *Integer and Combinatorial Optimization.* [19.5]
   Nesbitt, Cecil J. *Mathematics of Compound Interest.* [17.5]
   Nesher, Pearla. *Mathematics and Cognition.* [5.3]
   Neugebauer, O. *The Exact Sciences in Antiquity.* [3.5]
 * Newbold, Paul. *Statistics for Business and Economics.* [17.3]
 * Newell, Virginia K. *Black Mathematicians and Their Works.* [5.10]
** Newman, Claire M. *Exploring Probability.* [20.1]
** Newman, James R. *Gödel's Proof.* [9.2]
*** ———. *The World of Mathematics.* [1.1]
 * Nievergelt, Jurg. *Combinatorial Algorithms: Theory and Practice.* [22.8]
 * Nievergelt, Yves. *Mathematics in Business Administration.* [17.2]
 * Ninestein, Eleanor H. *Introduction to Computer Mathematics.* [16.4]
*** Niven, Ivan M. *An Introduction to the Theory of Numbers.* [11.1]
 * ———. *Irrational Numbers.* [11.2]
*** ———. *Mathematics of Choice or How to Count Without Counting.* [10.3]
*** ———. *Maxima and Minima Without Calculus.* [1.2]
*** ———. *Numbers: Rational and Irrational.* [11.2]
   Noble, Ben. *Applied Linear Algebra.* [12.1]
 * ———. *Applications of Undergraduate Mathematics in Engineering.* [24.1]
   Noether, Gottfried. *Introduction to Statistics: A Fresh Approach.* [21.2]

*** North Carolina School of Science. *Contemporary Precalculus Through Applications.* [6.2]
   Northrop, Eugene P. *Riddles in Mathematics: A Book of Paradoxes.* [4.3]
   Nustad, Harry L. *Essentials of Technical Mathematics.* [16.1]
   Nyman, Carl J. *Problems for General Chemistry and Qualitative Analysis.* [16.6]

O

   Oakley, C.O. *Principles of Mathematics.* [6.1]
** Oberg, Eric. *Machinery's Handbook.* [16.2]
** Obremski, Thomas E. *Exploring Probability.* [20.1]
** O'Daffer, Phares G. *Geometry: An Investigative Approach.* [14.3]
   ———. *How To Evaluate Progress in Problem Solving.* [5.11]
   Ogilvy, C. Stanley. *Excursions in Number Theory.* [11.2]
   ———. *A Calculus Notebook.* [6.5]
** ———. *Tomorrow's Math: Unsolved Problems for the Amateur.* [4.1]
   Oldham, Keith B. *An Atlas of Functions.* [2.2]
 * Olds, C.D. *Continued Fractions.* [11.3]
** Olinick, Michael. *An Introduction to Mathematical Models in the Social and Life Sciences.* [25.1]
   Olivo, C. Thomas. *Basic Vocational-Technical Mathematics.* [16.2]
   Olivo, Thomas P. *Basic Vocational-Technical Mathematics.* [16.2]
*** Olmsted, John M.H. *Theorems and Counterexamples in Mathematics.* [8.2]
 * Olver, F.W.J. *Asymptotics and Special Functions.* [8.6]
   O'Nan, Michael. *Linear Algebra.* [12.1]
   O'Neill, Barrett. *Elementary Differential Geometry.* [14.7]
   Ore, Oystein. *Cardano: The Gambling Scholar.* [3.2]
*** ———. *Graphs and Their Uses.* [10.4]
** ———. *Invitation to Number Theory.* [11.2]
   ———. *Niels Henrik Abel: Mathematician Extraordinary.* [3.2]
** ———. *Number Theory and Its History.* [11.3]
   O'Rourke, Joseph. *Art Gallery Theorems and Algorithms.* [14.6]
 * Orr, Eleanor Wilson. *Twice As Less: Black English and the Performance of Black Students in Mathematics and Science.* [5.10]
 * Osen, L.M. *Women in Mathematics.* [5.10]
   Oster, George F. *Caste and Ecology in the Social Insects.* [23.2]
 * Ott, Lyman. *Elementary Survey Sampling.* [21.7]

P

*** Packel, Edward W. *The Mathematics of Games and Gambling.* [20.1]
** Page, Warren. *Two-Year College Mathematics Readings.* [1.6]

Pakin, Sandra. *APL: The Language and Its Usage.* [22.7]

Palmer, Claude I. *Practical Mathematics.* [16.2]

* Papert, Seymour. *Mindstorms: Children, Computers, and Powerful Ideas.* [5.14]

————. *Perceptrons: An Introduction to Computational Geometry.* [22.11]

Parmenter, Michael M. *Theory of Interest and Life Contingencies with Pension Applications: A Problem Solving Approach.* [17.7]

Parsons, Torrence D. *Mathematical Methods in Finance and Economics.* [25.2]

Pasahow, Edward. *Mathematics for Electronics.* [16.5]

** Patashnik, Oren. *Concrete Mathematics: A Foundation for Computer Science.* [10.3]

Paul, Richard S. *Essentials of Technical Mathematics.* [16.1]

* Paulos, John Allen. *Beyond Numeracy: Ruminations of a Numbers Man.* [1.2]

————. *Innumeracy: Mathematical Illiteracy and Its Consequences.* [1.2]

Payne, Joseph N. *Mathematics For the Young Child.* [5.7]

————. *Advanced Mathematics: A Preparation for Calculus.* [6.2]

Pearson, Carl E. *Handbook of Applied Mathematics: Selected Results and Methods.* [24.1]

Peck, Roxy. *Statistics: The Exploration and Analysis of Data.* [21.2]

* Pedersen, Jean. *Build Your Own Polyhedra.* [14.5]

Pedoe, Dan. *Circles: A Mathematical View.* [14.4]

* ————. *Geometry and the Visual Arts.* [14.2]

————. *The Gentle Art of Mathematics.* [1.2]

Pedrick, George. *A First Course in Functional Analysis.* [8.5]

** Peitgen, Heinz-Otto. *The Beauty of Fractals: Images of Complex Dynamical Systems.* [8.3]

————. *The Science of Fractal Images.* [8.3]

* Penney, David E. *Elementary Differential Equations with Applications.* [7.1]

Penrose, Roger. *The Emperor's New Mind: Concerning Computers, Minds, and The Laws of Physics.* [1.2]

Pentakainen, T. *Risk Theory.* [17.7]

Perl, T.H. *Math Equals.* [5.10]

Pesonen, E. *Risk Theory.* [17.7]

Peters, M.S. *Elementary Chemical Engineering.* [16.6]

** Peterson, Ivars. *Islands of Truth.* [1.2]

** ————. *The Mathematical Tourist: Snapshots of Modern Mathematics.* [1.2]

Peterson, John C. *Math for the Automotive Trade.* [16.2]

* Phelps, E.R. *Practical Shop Mathematics.* [16.2]

Phillips, Esther R. *Studies in the History of Mathematics.* [3.1]

Phillips, Gary. *A World of Differences: An International Assessment of Mathematics and Science.* [5.13]

* Phillips, Hubert. *My Best Puzzles in Logic and Reasoning.* [4.3]

* ————. *My Best Puzzles in Mathematics.* [4.3]

Piaget, Jean. *The Child's Conception of Geometry.* [5.3]

* ————. *The Child's Conception of Number.* [5.3]

** Pickar, Gloria D. *Dosage Calculations.* [16.3]

Pike, Rob. *The UNIX Programming Environment.* [22.10]

Pinter, Charles C. *A Book of Abstract Algebra.* [13.1]

* Place, C.M. *An Introduction to Dynamical Systems.* [7.2]

*** Plauger, P.J. *The Elements of Programming Style.* [22.6]

Polimeni, Albert D. *Foundations of Discrete Mathematics.* [10.1]

Polivka, Raymond. *APL: The Language and Its Usage.* [22.7]

Pollack, Seymour V. *Studies in Computer Science.* [22.3]

* Pollard, Harry. *The Theory of Algebraic Numbers.* [11.5]

* ————. *Mathematical Introduction to Celestial Mechanics.* [24.5]

Pollard, J.H. *Introductory Statistics with Applications in General Insurance.* [17.3]

————. *Mathematical Models for the Growth of Human Populations.* [23.5]

Pólya, George. *Complex Variables.* [8.4]

*** ————. *How To Solve It.* [5.11]

————. *Inequalities.* [8.6]

** ————. *Mathematical Discovery: On Understanding, Learning, and Teaching Problem Solving.* [5.11]

** ————. *Mathematical Methods in Science.* [24.1]

* ————. *Mathematics and Plausible Reasoning.* [5.11]

————. *The Pólya Picture Album.* [3.6]

Pomerance, Carl. *Lecture Notes on Primality Testing and Factoring: A Short Course at Kent State University.* [11.4]

** Port, Dan. *Differential Equations: Theory and Applications.* [7.1]

Porter, Stuart R. *Basic Technical Mathematics with Calculus.* [16.7]

Post, Thomas R. *Teaching Mathematics in Grades K–8: Research Based Methods.* [5.7]

* Poston, Tim. *Catastrophe Theory and its Applications.* [19.2]

Power, Thomas C. *Electronics Mathematics.* [16.5]

Press, William H. *Numerical Recipes: The Art of Scientific Computing.* [18.5]

Pressman, R. *Software Engineering: A Practitioner's Approach.* [22.12]

*** Prichett, Gordon D. *Mathematics with Applications in Management and Economics.* [17.6]

** Priestley, William M. *Calculus: An Historical Approach.* [6.3]

Proschan, Frank. *The Statistical Exorcist: Dispelling Statistics Anxiety.* [21.1]

Protter, Murray H. *A First Course in Real Analysis.* [8.2]

Provine, W. *The Origins of Theoretical Population Genetics.* [23.4]

Prusinkiewicz, Przemyslaw. *Lindenmayer Systems, Fractals, and Plants.* [23.2]

Pugh, Anthony. *Polyhedra: A Visual Approach.* [14.5]

R

Rabinowitz, Philip. *A First Course in Numerical Analysis.* [18.1]

* ———. *Methods of Numerical Integration.* [18.1]

Rademacher, Hans. *The Enjoyment of Mathematics.* [1.2]

** ———. *Higher Mathematics from an Elementary Point of View.* [1.2]

Rader, Carl. *Fundamentals of Electronics Mathematics.* [16.5]

** Raiffa, Howard. *Games and Decisions.* [19.3]

Ralston, Anthony. *A First Course in Numerical Analysis.* [18.1]

———. *The Future of College Mathematics.* [5.9]

———. *Discrete Mathematics in the First Two Years.* [5.9]

* ———. *Discrete Algorithmic Mathematics.* [10.1]

Ranucci, E.R. *Creating Escher-Type Drawings.* [14.5]

Rao, C. Radhkirshna. *Linear Statistical Inference and Its Applications.* [21.4]

Rapoport, Anatol. *Mathematical Models in the Social and Behavioral Sciences.* [25.1]

Redfern, E.J. *Introduction to Number Theory with Computing.* [11.1]

** Redheffer, Ray. *Differential Equations: Theory and Applications.* [7.1]

Reed, Michael. *Methods of Modern Mathematical Physics.* [24.3]

** Reid, Constance. *Hilbert.* [3.2]

———. *International Mathematical Congresses: An Illustrated History, 1893–1986.* [3.6]

* Reingold, Edward M. *Combinatorial Algorithms: Theory and Practice.* [22.8]

* Reiter, Stanley. *Studies in Mathematical Economics.* [25.2]

** Remmert, Reinhold. *Theory of Complex Functions.* [8.4]

* Rényi, Alfréd. *A Diary on Information Theory.* [24.6]

* Resnick, Lauren B. *The Psychology of Mathematics for Instruction.* [5.3]

———. *Toward the Thinking Curriculum: Current Cognitive Research.* [5.12]

*** ———. *Education and Learning to Think.* [5.12]

Ribenboim, Paulo. *The Book of Prime Number Records.* [11.4]

** ———. *The Little Book of Big Primes.* [11.4]

Rice, Harold S. *Technical Mathematics with Calculus.* [16.7]

Rice, Jane. *Medications and Mathematics for the Nurse.* [16.3]

Rice, John R. *Matrix Computations and Mathematical Software.* [18.3]

* Richardson, Judith K. *The Mathematics of Drugs and Solutions with Clinical Applications.* [16.3]

* Richardson, Lloyd I. *The Mathematics of Drugs and Solutions with Clinical Applications.* [16.3]

Richmond, A.E. *Calculus for Electronics.* [16.5]

** Richter, P.H. *The Beauty of Fractals: Images of Complex Dynamical Systems.* [8.3]

Riesz, Frigyes. *Functional Analysis.* [8.5]

Riner, John. *Mathematics of Finance.* [17.5]

Ripley, Brian D. *Stochastic Simulation.* [19.5]

Rippon, P.J. *Microcomputers and Mathematics.* [22.1]

* Ritchie, Dennis M. *The C Programming Language.* [22.7]

** Robbins, H. *What is Mathematics?* [1.2]

Robbins, Omer, Jr. *Tonic Reactions and Equilibria.* [16.6]

Roberts, A. Wayne. *Faces of Mathematics: An Introductory Course for College Students.* [1.4]

* Roberts, Fred S. *Discrete and System Models.* [19.2]

———. *Applied Combinatorics.* [10.3]

* ———. *Discrete Mathematical Models with Applications to Social, Biological, and Environmental Problems.* [19.2]

———. *Graph Theory and Its Applications to Problems of Society.* [25.1]

Roberts, Keith. *Mathematics for Health Sciences.* [16.3]

Roberts, Paul M. *Mathematical Writing.* [5.9]

Robertson, John S. *Differential Equations with Applications and Historical Notes.* [7.1]

* Robinson, Abraham. *Non-standard Analysis.* [8.6]

———. *Numbers and Ideals.* [13.4]

Robson, David. *Smalltalk-80: The Language.* [22.7]

*** Rodi, Stephen B. *New Directions in Two-Year College Mathematics.* [5.9]

Rolfsen, Dale. *Knots and Links.* [15.2]

Roman, Steven. *An Introduction to Discrete Mathematics.* [10.1]

Romano, Joseph P. *Counterexamples in Probability and Statistics.* [20.6]

* Romberg, Thomas A. *Mathematics Assessment and Evaluation: Imperatives for Mathematics Educators.* [5.13]

Rorres, Chris. *Applications of Linear Algebra.* [12.1]

Rosenfeld, B.A. *A History of Non-Euclidean Geometry: Evolution of the Concept of a Geometric Space.* [3.9]

* Ross, Kenneth A. *Discrete Mathematics.* [10.1]

* ———. *Elementary Analysis: The Theory of Calculus.* [8.2]

Ross, Sheldon M. *Introduction to Probability Models.* [20.2]

* Roszak, Theodore. *The Cult of Information: The Folklore of Computers and the True Art of Thinking.* [22.2]

Rota, Gian-Carlo. *Discrete Thoughts: Essays on Mathematics, Science, and Philosophy.* [1.3]

———. *Ordinary Differential Equations.* [7.2]

Rothschild, V. *Probability Distributions.* [20.3]

* Rotman, Joseph J. *An Introduction to the Theory of Groups.* [13.3]

Rourke, Robert E.K. *Beginning Statistics with Data Analysis.* [21.5]

Rousos, T.G. *Mathematics for Business and New Consumers.* [17.1]

Rowe, David E. *The History of Modern Mathematics.* [3.1]

Royden, H.L. *Real Analysis.* [8.2]

Rubinstein, Moshe F. *Patterns of Problem Solving.* [5.11]

Rubinstein, Reuven Y. *Simulation and the Monte Carlo Method.* [19.5]

* Rucker, Rudy. *Geometry, Relativity, and the Fourth Dimension.* [14.1]

Ruckle, W.H. *Geometric Games and Their Applications.* [19.3]

Ruderman, Harry D. *NYSML-ARML Contests, 1973–1985.* [4.4]

** Rudin, Walter. *Principles of Mathematical Analysis.* [8.2]

———. *Real and Complex Analysis.* [8.4]

** Rudolph, William B. *Business Mathematics for College Students.* [17.1]

Russell, Bertrand. *The Autobiography of Bertrand Russell.* [3.2]

Ryser, H.J. *Combinatorial Mathematics.* [10.3]

S

Saaty, Thomas L. *Thinking With Models: Mathematical Models in the Physical, Biological, and Social Sciences.* [19.2]

———. *Nonlinear Mathematics.* [19.5]

———. *The Four-Color Problem: Assaults and Conquest.* [10.4]

*** Saber, John C. *Mathematics with Applications in Management and Economics.* [17.6]

Sahni, Sartaj. *Fundamentals of Data Structures in Pascal.* [22.4]

** Salkind, Charles T. *Contest Problem Book.* [4.4]

Sammons, Vivian O. *Blacks in Science and Medicine.* [5.10]

Samuel, Pierre. *Commutative Algebra.* [13.6]

Saunders, Hal M. *Mathematics for the Trades: A Guided Approach.* [16.2]

Saupe, Dietmar. *The Science of Fractal Images.* [8.3]

Savage, Katherine. *Nursing Simplified: Math Logic.* [16.3]

Savage, Leonard J. *Inequalities for Stochastic Processes (How to Gamble If You Must).* [20.4]

Sawyer, W.W. *Introducing Mathematics.* [1.3]

*** ———. *What is Calculus About?* [6.5]

* Schaaf, William L. *A Bibliography of Recreational Mathematics.* [2.4]

———. *Mathematics and Science: An Adventure in Postage Stamps.* [2.4]

Schaefer, Barbara K. *Using the Mathematical Literature: A Practical Guide.* [2.4]

*** Schattschneider, Doris J. *Visions of Symmetry: Notebooks, Periodic Drawings, and Related Work of M.C. Escher.* [14.5]

** Scheaffer, Richard L. *The Art and Techniques of Simulation.* [20.1]

* ———. *Elementary Survey Sampling.* [21.7]

** ———. *Exploring Probability.* [20.1]

** ———. *Introduction to Probability and Its Applications.* [20.2]

———. *Mathematical Statistics with Applications.* [21.4]

* Schell, Frank R. *Practical Problems in Mathematics for Welders.* [16.2]

** Schey, H.M. *Div, Grad, Curl, and All That: An Informal Text on Vector Calculus.* [6.4]

Schiffer, M.M. *The Role of Mathematics in Science.* [1.3]

* Schlesinger, B. *Thinking Through Mathematics: Fostering Inquiry and Communication in Mathematics Classrooms.* [5.6]

* Schneider, David I. *Finite Mathematics and Its Applications.* [10.2]

* ———. *Calculus and Its Applications.* [6.3]

Schoen, Harold L. *Estimation and Mental Computation: 1986 Yearbook.* [5.6]

Schoenberg, I.J. *Mathematical Time Exposures.* [1.2]

** Schoenfeld, Alan H. *A Sourcebook for College Mathematics Teaching.* [5.9]

———. *Cognitive Science and Mathematics Education.* [5.3]

** ———. *Mathematical Problem Solving.* [5.11]

* ———. *Problem Solving in the Mathematics Curriculum: A Report, Recommendations, and an Annotated Bibliography.* [5.11]

Schrage, Linus E. *A Guide to Simulation.* [19.5]

Schroeder, Manfred R. *Fractals, Chaos, Power Laws: Minutes from an Infinite Paradise.* [8.3]

———. *Number Theory in Science and Communication with Applications in Cryptography, Physics, Digital Information, Computing, and Self-Similarity.* [11.2]

Schwartz, Jacob T. *Discrete Thoughts: Essays on Mathematics, Science, and Philosophy.* [1.3]

* Scientific American. *Mathematics in the Modern World.* [1.1]

Scott, W.F. *An Introduction to the Mathematics of Finance.* [17.5]

Scudo, F. *The Golden Age of Theoretical Ecology.* [23.2]

* Sedgewick, Robert. *Algorithms in C.* [22.8]

* Seebach, J. Arthur, Jr. *Mathematics Magazine: 50 Year Index.* [2.5]

* ———. *Counterexamples in Topology.* [15.1]

Segel, Lee A. *Mathematics Applied to Deterministic Problems in the Natural Sciences.* [24.3]

———. *Modeling Dynamic Phenomena in Molecular and Cellular Biology.* [23.6]

Seidenberg, A. *Studies in Algebraic Geometry.* [14.7]

* Semendyayev, K.A. *Handbook of Mathematics.* [2.2]

* Senechal, Lester. *Models for Undergraduate Research in Mathematics.* [5.9]

* Senechal, Marjorie. *Shaping Space: A Polyhedral Approach.* [14.5]

** Sethi, Ravi. *Compilers: Principles, Techniques, and Tools.* [22.13]

Sewell, Granville. *The Numerical Solution of Ordinary and Partial Differential Equations.* [18.2]

Seymour, Dale. *Visual Patterns in Pascal's Triangle.* [6.1]

Shaevel, M. Leonard. *Essentials of Technical Mathematics.* [16.1]

* Sharpe, David. *Rings and Factorization.* [13.4]

** Shephard, G.C. *Tilings and Patterns.* [14.5]

* Shulte, Albert P. *New Directions for Elementary School Mathematics: 1989 Yearbook.* [5.7]

———. *Teaching Statistics and Probability: 1981 Yearbook.* [5.6]

* ———. *Learning and Teaching Geometry, K–12: 1987 Yearbook.* [5.6]

* ———. *The Ideas of Algebra, K–12: 1988 Yearbook.* [5.8]

Shumate, K. *Understanding Ada with Abstract Data Types.* [22.7]

Siegel, Andrew F. *Counterexamples in Probability and Statistics.* [20.6]

* Siegel, Martha J. *Finite Mathematics and Its Applications.* [10.2]

* Sierpiński, W. *250 Problems in Elementary Number Theory.* [11.3]

* Sigler, L.E. *Leonardo Pisano Fibonacci: The Book of Squares.* [3.4]

Silberschatz, Abraham. *Database System Concepts.* [22.5]

* Silver, Edward A. *The Teaching and Assessing of Mathematical Problem Solving.* [5.12]

* ———. *Thinking Through Mathematics: Fostering Inquiry and Communication in Mathematics Classrooms.* [5.6]

Silverman, David L. *Your Move.* [4.3]

Simmons, Donald M. *Nonlinear Programming for Operations Research.* [19.5]

Simmons, George F. *Differential Equations with Applications and Historical Notes.* [7.1]

———. *Calculus with Analytic Geometry.* [6.3]

* ———. *Introduction to Topology and Modern Analysis.* [15.1]

———. *Precalculus Mathematics in a Nutshell: Geometry, Algebra, Trigonometry.* [6.2]

Simon, Barry. *Methods of Modern Mathematical Physics.* [24.3]

Simpson, F. Morgan. *Activities for Junior High School and Middle School Mathematics.* [5.8]

*** Singer, B.B. *Basic Mathematics for Electricity and Electronics.* [16.5]

* Singer, I.M. *Lecture Notes on Elementary Topology and Geometry.* [15.4]

Siret, Y. *Computer Algebra: Systems and Algorithms for Algebraic Computation.* [22.8]

Skelley, Esther G. *Medications and Mathematics for the Nurse.* [16.3]

* Skemp, Richard R. *The Psychology of Learning Mathematics.* [5.3]

* Slater, Jeffrey. *Practical Business Math Procedures.* [17.1]

* Sloane, N.J.A. *A Handbook of Integer Sequences.* [2.2]

Slovic, Paul. *Judgment Under Uncertainty: Heuristics and Biases.* [20.1]

* Smale, Stephen. *Differential Equations, Dynamical Systems, and Linear Algebra.* [7.2]

Small, Donald B. *Calculus: An Integrated Approach.* [6.3]

———. *Explorations in Calculus with a Computer Algebra System.* [6.3]

Smart, James R. *Modern Geometries.* [14.2]

Smith, D. *A Transition to Advanced Mathematics.* [8.1]

** Smith, David A. *Computers and Mathematics: The Use of Computers in Undergraduate Instruction.* [5.9]

* Smith, David Eugene. *The Geometry of René Descartes.* [3.4]

** ———. *A Source Book in Mathematics.* [3.3]

* ———. *History of Mathematics.* [3.1]

** Smith, D.P. *Mathematical Demography.* [23.5]

Smith, H. *Applied Regression Analysis.* [21.6]

** Smith, J. Maynard. *Evolution and the Theory of Games.* [23.4]

———. *Models in Ecology.* [23.2]

Smith, Karl A. *How to Model It: Problem Solving for the Computer Age.* [19.2]

Smith, Karl J. *Finite Mathematics.* [10.2]

———. *Mathematics, Its Power and Utility.* [1.4]

———. *The Nature of Mathematics.* [1.4]

Smith, Larry. *Linear Algebra.* [12.1]

Smith, Loretta M. *Clinical Calculations: A Unified Approach.* [16.3]

Smith, Martha K. *Emmy Noether: A Tribute to Her Life and Work.* [3.2]

Smith, Peter D. *Graded Problems in Computer Science.* [22.3]

*** Smith, Robert D. *Mathematics for Machine Technology.* [16.2]

* ———. *Vocational-Technical Mathematics.* [16.1]

Smullyan, Raymond M. *The Lady or the Tiger? And Other Logic Puzzles.* [4.3]

Sneddon, I.N. *Encyclopedic Dictionary of Mathematics for Engineers and Applied Scientists.* [2.1]

** Snedecor, George W. *Statistical Methods.* [21.4]

** Snell, J. Laurie. *Introduction to Finite Mathematics.* [10.2]

———. *Finite Markov Chains.* [20.4]

** ———. *Introduction to Probability.* [20.2]

———. *Mathematical Models in the Social Sciences.* [25.1]

———. *Random Walks and Electric Networks.* [20.4]

Snyder, Henry D. *Topics for Mathematics Clubs.* [5.8]

Sobel, Max A. *Algebra and Trigonometry: A Pre-Calculus Approach.* [6.2]

* ———. *Readings for Enrichment in Secondary School Mathematics.* [5.8]

Sobel, M.J. *Handbook in Operations Research and Management Science.* [19.5]

Sobol, I.M. *The Monte Carlo Method.* [20.4]

Sobolev, V. *Elements of Functional Analysis.* [8.5]

** Solow, Daniel. *How To Read and Do Proofs: An Introduction to Mathematical Thought Processes.* [8.1]

Sommerville, Ian. *Software Engineering.* [22.12]

Southwick, Charles E. *Practical Problems in Mathematics for Graphic Arts.* [16.2]

Spanier, Jerome. *An Atlas of Functions.* [2.2]

Spence, Lawrence E. *Applied Mathematics for the Management, Life, and Social Sciences.* [17.2]

* Spirer, Herbert F. *Misused Statistics: Straight Talk for Twisted Numbers.* [21.1]

Spivak, Michael D. *The Joy of TEX: A Gourmet Guide to Typesetting with the AMS-TEX Macro Package.* [22.15]

Springer, C.H. *Mathematics for Management Sciences.* [17.6]

Stacey, Kaye. *Thinking Mathematically.* [5.11]

** Stancl, Donald L. *Calculus for Management and the Life and Social Sciences.* [17.4]

** ———. *Mathematics for the Management and the Life and Social Sciences.* [17.2]

** Stancl, Mildred L. *Calculus for Management and the Life and Social Sciences.* [17.4]

** ———. *Mathematics for the Management and the Life and Social Sciences.* [17.2]

St. Andre, R. *A Transition to Advanced Mathematics.* [8.1]

Starfield, Anthony M. *How to Model It: Problem Solving for the Computer Age.* [19.2]

* Starr, Ross M. *General Equilibrium Models of Monetary Economics: Studies in the Static Foundation of Monetary Theory.* [25.2]

Steen, Lynn Arthur. *Teaching Teachers, Teaching Students: Reflections on Mathematical Education.* [5.6]

* ———. *Counterexamples in Topology.* [15.1]

* ———. *Mathematics Magazine: 50 Year Index.* [2.5]

*** ———. *Calculus for a New Century: A Pump, Not a Filter.* [5.9]

** ———. *Mathematics Today: Twelve Informal Essays.* [1.1]

* ———. *Mathematics Tomorrow.* [1.1]

*** ———. *On the Shoulders of Giants: New Approaches to Numeracy.* [5.1]

** ———. *Annotated Bibliography of Expository Writing in the Mathematical Sciences.* [2.4]

*** Steenrod, Norman E. *First Concepts of Topology.* [15.1]

* Stehney, Ann K. *Selected Papers on Geometry.* [14.2]

** Stein, Sherman K. *Calculus and Analytic Geometry.* [6.3]

———. *Mathematics, The Man-made Universe: An Introduction to the Spirit of Mathematics.* [1.4]

Steinhaus, Hugo. *Mathematical Snapshots.* [1.2]

** Sterrett, Andrew. *Using Writing to Teach Mathematics.* [5.9]

Stevenson, Harold W. *Making the Grade in Mathematics: Elementary School Mathematics in the United States, Taiwan, and Japan.* [5.13]

———. *Mathematical Knowledge of Japanese, Chinese, and American Elementary School Children.* [5.13]

Stewart, Ian. *Algebraic Number Theory.* [11.5]

* ———. *Catastrophe Theory and its Applications.* [19.2]

* ———. *Concepts of Modern Mathematics.* [1.2]

* ———. *Does God Play Dice? The Mathematics of Chaos.* [1.2]

———. *Game, Set, and Math: Enigmas and Conundrums.* [4.2]

* ———. *The Problems of Mathematics.* [1.2]

Stigler, James W. *Mathematical Knowledge of Japanese, Chinese, and American Elementary School Children.* [5.13]

*** Stigler, Stephen M. *The History of Statistics: The Measurement of Uncertainty Before 1900.* [3.10]

Stillwell, John. *Mathematics and Its History.* [3.1]

*** Stoll, Clifford. *The Cuckoo's Egg: Tracking a Spy Through the Maze of Computer Espionage.* [22.2]

** Straffin, Philip D., Jr. *Political and Related Models.* [25.3]

———. *Topics in the Theory of Voting.* [25.3]

Straight, H. Joseph. *Foundations of Discrete Mathematics.* [10.1]

** Strang, Gilbert. *Calculus.* [6.3]

** ———. *Introduction to Applied Mathematics.* [24.2]

** ———. *Linear Algebra and Its Applications.* [12.1]

Stromberg, Karl R. *Real and Abstract Analysis: A Modern Treatment of the Theory of Functions of a Real Variable.* [8.2]

* Stroup, Donna F. *Statistics in the Real World: A Book of Examples.* [21.3]

Struik, Dirk Jan. *A Source Book in Mathematics, 1200–1800.* [3.3]

* ———. *A Concise History of Mathematics.* [3.1]

Stubbs, David F. *Data Structures.* [22.4]

Sullivan, Michael. *Finite Mathematics with Applications for Business and Social Sciences.* [17.2]

Sullivan, Richard L. *Modern Electronics Mathematics.* [16.5]

** ———. *Practical Problems in Mathematics for Electronics Technicians.* [16.5]

** Sussman, Gerald J. *Structure and Interpretation of Computer Programs.* [22.3]

** Sussman, Julie. *Structure and Interpretation of Computer Programs.* [22.3]

* Sutton, O.G. *Mathematics in Action.* [24.1]

Swaine, Michael. *Fire in the Valley: The Making of the Personal Computer.* [3.11]

Swann, Howard. *Prof. E. McSquared's Expanded Intergalactic Version: A Calculus Primer.* [6.5]

Swetz, Frank J. *Was Pythagoras Chinese? An Examination of Right Triangle Theory in Ancient China.* [3.5]

———. *Capitalism and Arithmetic: The New Math of the 15th Century.* [3.4]

** Swift, Jim. *Exploring Surveys and Information From Samples.* [21.1]

** ———. *The Art and Techniques of Simulation.* [20.1]

Swokowski, Earl W. *Algebra and Trigonometry with Analytic Geometry.* [6.2]

———. *Calculus.* [6.3]

Szebehely, Victor G. *Adventures in Celestial Mechanics: A First Course in the Theory of Orbits.* [24.5]

Székely, Gábor J. *Paradoxes in Probability Theory and Mathematical Statistics.* [20.6]

Szeminska, A. *The Child's Conception of Geometry.* [5.3]

T

Tall, David. *Algebraic Number Theory.* [11.5]

Tan, S.T. *Applied Finite Mathematics.* [10.2]

* Tanenbaum, Andrew S. *Structured Computer Organization.* [22.15]

* Tanis, Elliot A. *Probability and Statistical Inference.* [21.4]

*** Tanur, Judith M. *Statistics: A Guide to the Unknown.* [21.1]

*** ———. *Statistics: A Guide to Business and Economics.* [17.3]

*** ———. *Statistics: A Guide to Political and Social Issues.* [25.1]

*** ———. *Statistics: A Guide to the Study of the Biological and Health Sciences.* [23.1]

Taub, A.H. *Studies in Applied Mathematics.* [24.1]

Taylor, Howard M. *An Introduction to Stochastic Modeling.* [20.4]

Taylor, Ross. *Professional Development for Teachers of Mathematics: A Handbook.* [5.6]

Teeters, J.L. *Creating Escher-Type Drawings.* [14.5]

*** Thomas, George B., Jr. *Calculus and Analytic Geometry.* [6.3]

———. *Calculus.* [6.3]

** Thompson, Gerald L. *Introduction to Finite Mathematics.* [10.2]

** Thompson, Maynard. *Life Science Models.* [23.1]

* ———. *Finite Mathematics.* [10.2]

———. *Mathematical Models and Applications with Emphasis on the Social, Life, and Management Sciences.* [25.1]

** Thompson, Thomas M. *From Error-Correcting Codes Through Sphere Packings to Simple Groups.* [10.5]

Thorne, Kip S. *Gravitation.* [24.4]

Thoro, Dmitri. *Applied Combinatorics with Problem Solving.* [10.3]

* Thorpe, John A. *Lecture Notes on Elementary Topology and Geometry.* [15.4]

———. *Linear Algebra with Applications to Differential Equations.* [12.1]

* Thrall, Robert M. *Discrete and System Models.* [19.2]

Tietjen, Gary L. *A Topical Dictionary of Statistics.* [2.1]

* Tietze, Heinrich. *Famous Problems of Mathematics: Solved and Unsolved Mathematical Problems From Antiquity to Modern Times.* [1.3]

Tobias, Sheila. *Overcoming Math Anxiety.* [5.6]

———. *Succeed With Math: Every Student's Guide to Conquering Math Anxiety.* [5.6]

* ———. *They're Not Dumb, They're Different: Stalking the Second Tier.* [5.9]

* Toeplitz, Otto. *Calculus: A Genetic Approach.* [6.5]

———. *The Enjoyment of Mathematics.* [1.2]

* Topper, Michael A. *Mathematics for Technical Education.* [16.7]

* ———. *Technical Calculus.* [16.7]

Tournier, E. *Computer Algebra: Systems and Algorithms for Algebraic Computation.* [22.8]

* Trafton, Paul R. *New Directions for Elementary School Mathematics: 1989 Yearbook.* [5.7]

Tremblay, Jean-Paul. *Theory and Practice of Compiler Writing.* [22.13]

* Triola, Mario F. *Introduction to Technical Mathematics.* [16.1]

* Tromba, Anthony J. *Mathematics and Optimal Form.* [14.1]

Trotter, Hale F. *Calculus of Vector Functions.* [6.4]

Trowbridge, Charles L. *Fundamental Concepts of Actuarial Science.* [17.7]

* Tucker, Alan. *A Unified Introduction to Linear Algebra: Models, Methods, and Theory.* [12.1]

** ———. *Applied Combinatorics.* [10.3]

* Tucker, Allen B. *Fundamentals of Computing I: Logic, Problem-Solving, Programs, and Computers.* [22.3]

*** Tucker, Thomas W. *Priming the Calculus Pump: Innovations and Resources.* [5.9]

** Tufte, Edward R. *Envisioning Information.* [21.1]

*** ———. *The Visual Display of Quantitative Information.* [21.1]

* Tukey, John W. *Understanding Robust and Exploratory Data Analysis.* [21.5]

** ———. *Data Analysis and Regression: A Second Course in Statistics.* [21.6]

* Tversky, Amos. *Mathematical Psychology: An Elementary Introduction.* [25.4]

———. *Judgment Under Uncertainty: Heuristics and Biases.* [20.1]

U

** Ulam, S.M. *Adventures of a Mathematician.* [3.2]

** Ullman, Jeffrey D. *Compilers: Principles, Techniques, and Tools.* [22.13]

*** ———. *Data Structures and Algorithms.* [22.4]

** ———. *Introduction to Automata Theory, Languages, and Computation.* [22.15]

———. *Principals of Database and Knowledge-based Systems.* [22.5]

** ———. *The Design and Analysis of Computer Algorithms.* [22.8]

Usiskin, Zalman. *Advanced Algebra with Transformations and Applications.* [6.2]

V

Vajda, Steven. *Analysis.* [24.1]

van der Ploeg, Frederick. *Mathematical Methods in Economics.* [25.2]

** van der Waerden, B.L. *A History of Algebra: From al-Khwārizmī to Emmy Noether.* [3.7]

* ———. *Algebra.* [13.2]

———. *Geometry and Algebra in Ancient Civilizations.* [3.5]

* ———. *Science Awakening.* [3.5]

* Van Loan, Charles F. *Matrix Computations.* [18.3]

Vanden Eynden, Charles. *Applied Mathematics for the Management, Life, and Social Sciences.* [17.2]

Varberg, Dale E. *Faces of Mathematics: An Introductory Course for College Students.* [1.4]

Velleman, Paul F. *Applications, Basics, and Computing of Exploratory Data Analysis.* [21.5]

Vermeersch, LaVonne F. *Practical Problems in Mathematics for Graphic Arts.* [16.2]

Viète, François. *The Analytic Art.* [3.4]

** von Mises, Richard. *Probability, Statistics, and Truth.* [20.5]

* von Neumann, John. *The Computer and the Brain.* [22.1]

von Seggern, David H. *CRC Handbook of Mathematical Curves and Surfaces.* [2.2]

Vorob'ev, N.N. *Fibonacci Numbers.* [11.3]

W

Wackerly, Dennis D. *Mathematical Statistics with Applications.* [21.4]

** Wagner, Harvey M. *Principles of Operations Research with Applications to Managerial Decisions.* [19.1]

* Wagner, Sigrid. *Research Issues in the Learning and Teaching of Algebra.* [5.12]

Waite, William M. *Compiler Construction.* [22.13]

** Waits, Bert K. *Precalculus Mathematics—A Graphing Approach.* [6.2]

Wald, Robert M. *Space, Time, and Gravity: The Theory of the Big Bang and Black Holes.* [24.5]

Wall, Charles R. *Basic Technical Mathematics.* [16.1]

Walsh, J.E. *Numerical Algorithms.* [18.5]

Walter, Marion I. *The Art of Problem Posing.* [5.11]

Wan, Frederic Y.M. *Mathematical Models and Their Analysis.* [19.2]

Washburn, D.K. *Symmetries of Culture: Handbook of Plane Pattern Analysis.* [25.1]

* Washington, Allyn J. *Introduction to Technical Mathematics.* [16.1]

*** ———. *Basic Technical Mathematics with Calculus.* [16.7]

*** Watkins, Ann E. *New Directions in Two-Year College Mathematics.* [5.9]

** ———. *Exploring Data.* [21.1]

** ———. *Exploring Surveys and Information From Samples.* [21.1]

Watkins, J. *Graphs: An Introductory Approach.* [10.4]

* Watt, Alan. *Fundamentals of Three Dimensional Computer Graphics.* [22.14]

Weaver, Mabel E. *Programmed Mathematics of Drugs and Solutions.* [16.3]

** Weaver, Warren. *Lady Luck: The Theory of Probability.* [20.1]

Webre, Neil W. *Data Structures.* [22.4]

* Weeks, Jeffrey R. *The Shape of Space: How to Visualize Surfaces and Three-Dimensional Manifolds.* [15.2]

* Weil, André. *Number Theory: An Approach Through History From Hammurapi to Legendre.* [11.2]

** Weinstein, Alan. *Calculus III.* [6.4]

** ———. *Calculus.* [6.3]

* Weir, Maurice D. *A First Course in Mathematical Modeling.* [19.2]

Weisberg, Sanford. *Applied Linear Regression.* [21.6]

* Weiss, Eric A. *A Computer Science Reader: Selections from Abacus.* [22.1]

** Weizenbaum, Joseph. *Computer Power and Human Reason: From Judgment to Calculation.* [22.2]

Wenninger, Magnus J. *Spherical Models.* [14.5]

Wermer, John. *Linear Algebra Through Geometry.* [12.1]

Wesner, Terry H. *Essentials of Technical Mathematics.* [16.1]

West, Beverly H. *Differential Equations: A Dynamical Systems Approach.* [7.1]

** Westfall, Richard S. *Never at Rest: A Biography of Isaac Newton.* [3.2]

* Wexelblat, Richard L. *History of Programming Languages.* [22.6]

Weyuker, Elaine J. *Computability, Complexity, and Languages: Fundamentals of Theoretical Computer Science.* [22.9]

Wheatley, Patrick O. *Applied Numerical Analysis.* [18.1]

Wheeler, John Archibald. *Gravitation.* [24.4]

Whitehead, Alfred North. *An Introduction to Mathematics.* [1.2]

Whiteside, D.T. *The Mathematical Papers of Isaac Newton.* [3.4]

Whittaker, R.H. *Communities and Ecosystems.* [23.2]

Wichern, Dean W. *Applied Multivariate Statistical Analysis.* [21.8]

———. *Intermediate Business Statistics.* [17.3]

Wiener, Norbert. *Ex-Prodigy: My Childhood and Youth* and *I Am A Mathematician: Life of a Prodigy.* [3.2]

** Wiggins, Stephen. *Introduction to Applied Nonlinear Dynamical Systems and Chaos.* [7.2]

** Wilder, Raymond L. *Evolution of Mathematical Concepts: An Elementary Study.* [3.5]

Wilf, Herbert S. *Algorithms and Complexity.* [22.8]

Wilkinson, James H. *The Algebraic Eigenvalue Problem.* [18.3]

** Willard, Stephen. *General Topology.* [15.1]

* Williams, Bill. *A Sampler on Sampling.* [21.7]

Williams, H.P. *Model Building in Mathematical Programming.* [19.2]

* Williams, John D. *The Compleat Strategyst: Being a Primer on the Theory of Games of Strategy.* [19.3]

Williamson, Richard E. *Calculus of Vector Functions.* [6.4]

Wilson, Bruce. *Logical Nursing Mathematics.* [16.3]

Wilson, Edward O. *Caste and Ecology in the Social Insects.* [23.2]

Wilson, Robin J. *Graphs: An Introductory Approach.* [10.4]

———. *Graph Theory, 1736-1936.* [10.4]

Winfree, Arthur T. *The Geometry of Biological Time.* [23.6]

* ———. *The Timing of Biological Clocks.* [23.6]

Winn, P.R. *Quantitative Methods for Management.* [17.6]

Winograd, Shmuel. *Arithmetic Complexity of Computations.* [22.9]

* Winston, Patrick H. *Artificial Intelligence: An MIT Perspective.* [22.11]

* ———. *LISP.* [22.7]

** ———. *Artificial Intelligence.* [22.11]

Winston, Wayne L. *Operations Research: Applications and Algorithms.* [19.1]

* Wirth, Niklaus. *Algorithms and Data Structures.* [22.4]

* ———. *Programming in Modula-2.* [22.7]

* Witzke, Paul T. *Technical Mathematics I and II.* [16.1]

* Wolfe, John H. *Practical Shop Mathematics.* [16.2]

* Wolsey, Laurence A. *Integer and Combinatorial Optimization.* [19.5]

Wonnacott, Ronald J. *Econometrics.* [25.2]

Wonnacott, Thomas H. *Econometrics.* [25.2]

** Woodcock, Alexander. *Catastrophe Theory.* [19.2]

* Worth, Joan. *Preparing Elementary School Mathematics Teachers: Readings from the Arithmetic Teacher.* [5.7]

* Wright, Charles R.B. *Discrete Mathematics.* [10.1]

* Wright, E.M. *Introduction to the Theory of Numbers.* [11.3]

Wulf, William A. *Fundamental Structures of Computer Science.* [22.3]

Y

Yaglom, A.M. *Challenging Mathematical Programs with Elementary Solutions.* [4.4]

* ———. *Probability and Information.* [20.6]

Yaglom, I.M. *Challenging Mathematical Programs with Elementary Solutions.* [4.4]

** ———. *Geometric Transformations.* [14.8]

* ———. *Probability and Information.* [20.6]

* Yates, Robert C. *Curves and Their Properties.* [14.8]

* ———. *The Trisection Problem.* [14.4]

Youden, W.J. *Experimentation and Measurement.* [21.3]

* ———. *Risk, Choice, and Prediction: An Introduction to Experimentation.* [21.3]

Young, Gail S. *The Future of College Mathematics.* [5.9]

** Young, H. Peyton. *Fair Representation: Meeting the Ideal of One Man, One Vote.* [25.3]

Young, John Wesley. *Projective Geometry.* [14.8]

Z

Zadeh, Lotfi. *Linear Systems Theory.* [24.3]

Zariski, Oscar. *Commutative Algebra.* [13.6]

* Zaslavsky, Claudia. *Africa Counts: Number and Pattern in African Culture.* [5.4]

Zehnwirth, B. *Introductory Statistics with Applications in General Insurance.* [17.3]

Ziegler, J. *The Golden Age of Theoretical Ecology.* [23.2]

*** Ziegler, Michael R. *Applied Mathematics for Business, Economics, Life Sciences, and Social Sciences.* [17.2]

———. *Finite Mathematics for Management, Life, and Social Sciences.* [17.2]

* Zill, Dennis G. *A First Course in Differential Equations with Applications.* [7.1]

Zima, P. *Mathematics of Finance.* [17.5]

** Zimmermann, Walter. *Visualization in Teaching and Learning Mathematics.* [5.9]

*** Zuckerman, Herbert S. *An Introduction to the Theory of Numbers.* [11.1]

Zweng, Marilyn J. *Proceedings of the Fourth International Congress on Mathematical Education.* [5.6]

———. *Computers in Mathematics Education: 1984 Yearbook.* [5.14]

———. *Estimation and Mental Computation: 1986 Yearbook.* [5.06]

———. *The Secondary School Mathematics Curriculum: 1985 Yearbook.* [5.08]